PRAISE FOR

THE

OPPORTUNITY

AGENDA

"For far too long, the Democratic Party has relied on stale ideas, big government solutions, and uninspired messaging. Fisher and James show us that we can do better, proposing realistic policy changes with widespread voter appeal. This is the call to action the party needs."

HEIDI HEITKAMP
former senator (D-ND)

"The economic system in America used to reward hard work and generally provide for families. Now, that promise has completely evaporated. As Washington grapples with how to react, Winston Fisher and Sly James issue an urgent and needed warning: the Democratic Party is due for disruption. Now is the time to go big, go bold, and advance an agenda that spreads opportunity to everyone, everywhere."

JONATHAN COWAN
president, Third Way

"I'm often asked what Democrats need to do to broaden our appeal and win more elections. *The Opportunity Agenda* helps provide that answer. It shows the power of being proactive and how we need to continue to capture the economic agenda. Anyone looking for the path forward should read this book."

JIM MESSINA

CEO, Messina Group; campaign manager,
Obama for America 2012

"The central premise of *The Opportunity Agenda* is that to be successful as a party and a country, we need to offer a bold and innovative new policy agenda that appeals to a broad swath of Americans. NewDEAL works with forward-looking, pro-growth progressive state and local elected officials across the country. For them, and for every policymaker out there who believes that ideas matter, this book, and its actionable policy framework, will be both a breath of fresh air and an important resource."

DEBBIE COX BULTAN

CEO, NewDEAL (Developing Exceptional American Leaders)

"Sly is known for speaking plainly and helpfully about how public policy can improve people's lives. I'm not at all surprised to see he and Winston teamed up to push Democrats to look beyond today's news cycle and toward tomorrow's challenges. Agreement with every part of Sly and Winston's agenda is not required, as this book is the definition of thought-provoking. I suggest reading it with a pen in hand."

JASON KANDER

former Missouri secretary of state

"Sly James and Winston Fisher have a compelling message for Democrats in this critical election year: the key choice isn't between left and center, it's between old and new. To a party whose big government agenda has grown stale, *The Opportunity Agenda* offers a timely infusion of fresh ideas and a new approach to governing from the ground up."

WILL MARSHALL

president and founder, Progressive Policy Institute

www.amplifypublishing.com

For more information, please contact:
Amplify Publishing, an imprint of Mascot Books
620 Herndon Parkway #320
Herndon, VA 20170
info@amplifypublishing.com

Library of Congress Control Number: 2020906130

CPSIA Code: PRV0520A
ISBN-13: 978-1-64543-081-0

Printed in the United States

To my mother, Sandra, who instilled in me a deep sense of civic pride and an entrepreneurial attitude.

To my children, Kaia and Andrew. I hope this inspires you to speak up, make a difference, and challenge the status quo throughout your lives and in everything you do.

—WINSTON FISHER

This work is dedicated to our children who will inherit the sweet and bitter fruits of what we do and what we fail to do.

—SLY JAMES

THE
OPPORTUNITY
AGENDA

A Bold Democratic Plan
to Grow the Middle Class

WINSTON FISHER
AND SLY JAMES

CONTENTS

PREFACE AN OPPORTUNITY *FOR YOU*   XI

INTRODUCTION COMPELLING ANSWERS *FOR YOU*   1

CHAPTER 1 THE MOST IMPORTANT
YEARS OF OUR LIVES   17

CHAPTER 2 A SECOND REVOLUTION IN
AMERICAN EDUCATION   45

CHAPTER 3 "FIX THE DAMN ROADS"   75

CHAPTER 4 A PORTABLE SOCIAL CONTRACT   99

CHAPTER 5 EVERYDAY ENTREPRENEURS   125

CONCLUSION BEYOND THE REBOUND   153

ACKNOWLEDGMENTS   167

ABOUT THE AUTHORS   171

ENDNOTES   175

INDEX   199

PREFACE

AN OPPORTUNITY
FOR YOU

In ordinary times, political loyalties are relatively fixed. For many Americans, our choice of party and candidate is not open to question. It's just what we've always done. That's the reason why, in ordinary times, both parties spend so much energy riling up their respective bases. It's also why they go to such great lengths to win over a relatively few undecided voters in key swing states or districts, while writing off vast swaths of the electorate as "unwinnable."

These are not ordinary times. We are now facing an unprecedented economic crisis triggered by the COVID-19 pandemic and its aftermath. In 2020, it disrupted the world's health and economic norms with a vengeance. In the United States, it abruptly ended the extended period of global market growth that began under

President Obama and was the only business climate President Trump has ever known.

The pandemic not only exposed the glaring weaknesses of our domestic economy—it accelerated them. Before this crisis occurred, the pervasive wealth inequality and lack of opportunity for ordinary Americans was troublesome, to say the least, but ignorable by many. Now it is front and center.

This crisis creates an opportunity for strong leadership and great ideas—policies and programs that meet the needs of a broad swath of American voters. Had Democrats been successful in prioritizing and implementing the ideas outlined in this book, the economic impact of COVID-19 would have been far less. Access to capital for small businesses, for example, would have been an established norm instead of a hastily and inefficiently implemented emergency program. But it's not too late to take bold, decisive action. As we look forward, these policies would have a tremendous positive impact on our economic recovery.

This is a unique moment, one in which Democrats with the right ideas can appeal to dissatisfied independents and moderate Republicans for a generation or even longer. How we deal with the COVID-19 crisis, both in the short term and for years to come, will determine the success or failure of the American middle class and those seeking to enter the middle class in the twenty-first century.

THE WAY FORWARD

The massive recovery effort we face in the wake of the pandemic will require actions that appeal to a broad spectrum of Americans. The underlying problems identified in this book—and the solutions addressing them—are as true now as they were before the crisis. They are simply more urgent than ever.

In the past, there have been times when Congress and the president have accomplished great things, responding to crises with meaningful, sustainable policies and programs. Whether the crisis was economic, military, or both, our political leaders got big things done, and the American people applauded them for it. If that is to happen in response to COVID-19 and its aftermath, it will not be Donald Trump or his allies leading the charge or sparking the change.

At this moment, Americans are craving political leaders who are candid, focused on solutions, and clearly committed to getting things done. This is a unique opportunity for Democrats to appeal to voters outside their hard-core base. As the 2020 pandemic revealed, people are drawn to local officials who handle crises and disruptions with honesty and pragmatism. The same cannot be said of others charged with managing the crisis, particularly those lacking in candor and transparency or driven by ideological considerations.

Despite its tragic consequences, the COVID-19 crisis is an opportunity for creating real change. More than ever, the Democratic Party must become exactly that: the party of opportunity. It cannot merely represent a pendulum swing away from Donald Trump and his failures before and during the crisis. It must accomplish great things, facilitating policies that provide a ladder up to a wider swath of Americans. It must be the party of ideas that remain effective and compelling long after Donald Trump is out of office, and off the ballot.

THE OPPORTUNITY AGENDA

The purpose of this book is to outline a platform that speaks to economic anxieties that were decisive in recent elections but are even more pronounced in the post-COVID era. It will resonate with many Democrats, independents, and even some Republicans. It represents an agenda for voters demanding a chance to improve their current situation. The goal is not merely to woo disenfranchised working-class Americans to vote for a Democrat; it is to build a genuine, long-lasting coalition by building a platform that provides real opportunity for middle- and working-class American households.

For the foreseeable future, economic recovery will be front and center, in everyone's thoughts, and decisive in voters' choice of who will lead them forward. To be successful, the Democratic Party must represent such an agenda, one rooted in opportunity *for you, the broadest possible electorate.* This book explores five policy areas that constitute the pillars of a winning Democratic platform:

Childcare: School closings—including pre-K and public day care—in order to limit the spread of COVID-19 revealed astounding gaps in our childcare systems. Too many essential workers with young children or children with special needs at home were unable to afford help, even if day care or other support services stayed open.

As we recover from the pandemic, and as restrictions and layoffs abate, the need for effective, affordable childcare will be even more acute. The opportunity for meeting this need is spelled out in chapter 1. Rebuilding the economy will only happen if workers don't have to choose between having a job and supporting the well-being and healthy development of their children.

Education: Before the outbreak, and the widespread closure of public schools, a generation of students already was not receiving the skills needed to thrive in today's economy. The sudden transition to distance learning did not improve the situation, although it did reveal an unsettling digital divide along socioeconomic lines. In the COVID aftermath, too many students are falling even further behind.

As outlined in chapter 2, the opportunity for a revolution in education is clearly before us. The lessons of the pandemic must not be wasted. Rather than simply applying new technology to old programs, we need to fill the skills gap, not only for public schools and colleges but also for ongoing learning, retraining, and apprenticeship programs. In light of the economic realities faced by students and graduates, education policies and programs must work for more Americans.

Infrastructure: Chapter 3 provides a road map for Opportunity Democrats when it comes to rebuilding our country's infrastructure, including the potential for more effective public-private partnerships. The need for better roads, bridges, and railways—not to mention a modern power grid and wider access to the internet—has never been greater.

Not only can public-private partnerships help bridge budget gaps, they can also help drive the post-COVID economic recovery. Rather than give lip service to the value of infrastructure, it's time for Opportunity Democrats to give such programs the emphasis they deserve—to put more displaced workers back on the job.

Modern Benefits: The pandemic and its immediate business disruption caused a spike in unemployment never before seen in our country. Without warning, traditional, employer-supplied benefits disappeared for many, highlighting the growing workforce disparity, as well as the vulnerability of gig workers without access to traditional benefits, as discussed in chapter 4. However, the crisis also revealed an even greater, preexisting problem: the ongoing erosion of jobs (and their benefits) caused by automation. Under the current, outdated system, the fear of losing benefits is a big reason why Americans are reluctant to try for better careers or start new businesses.

As we recover, Opportunity Democrats must advocate for a new, portable, prorated, and universal approach to benefits—one that stays with the worker, not the job. In doing so, workers in the new economy, from small business startups to gig workers, as well as the temporarily unemployed, will benefit greatly over the long term. Given such tangible support and opportunity to thrive, many will become Democrats for life.

Entrepreneurship: American innovation, a common thread throughout history, was strongly in evidence during the pandemic and will be a major factor in powering our recovery. But the chief barrier to success—absence of sufficient capital—is still a formidable one. The pandemic brought to light the precarious financial state of too many small businesses. Even the relief program initiated in response to the crisis revealed the inherent difficulties faced by small businesses when navigating funding issues. Despite the political rhetoric, larger companies tended to get help more easily, while smaller businesses did not.

Chapter 5 of *The Opportunity Agenda* focuses on creating an entrepreneurial ecosystem that acknowledges that small businesses are the backbone of our economy and, in turn, provides them with the opportunity to achieve the American Dream. The goal is not to stick it to Republicans and their allies. Rather, it is a chance to create a deeper well of support for the majority of forward-thinking, creatively minded (and especially hardworking) Americans.

AN OPPORTUNITY *FOR YOU*

The COVID-19 pandemic is a tragedy whose medical, economic, and emotional costs are not yet fully known. But it is also a unique opportunity for Americans to pause and reflect on who we are, what we believe, and why. For Democrats, it's a chance to go beyond riling up the base and waiting for the pendulum to swing back in our favor. It is a genuine opportunity to broaden our electoral appeal, by solving problems and creating policies and programs of lasting value and opportunity for all Americans. The silver lining in this very dark cloud is the Democratic Party's opportunity to create a platform that delivers *for you!*

COMPELLING

ANSWERS *FOR YOU*

CATCHING THE REBOUND

For Democrats, it's both the worst of times and, by some measure, our most hopeful moment in a decade.

We may not control the White House, the Senate, or the Supreme Court for the time being. But the public's decidedly mixed reaction to President Trump (we're doing our best to be generous here) combined with a Republican agenda that alienates huge swaths of the electorate, points to a seemingly inevitable Democratic renaissance. If the results of the 2018 midterm elections offer a window into how future contests are likely to turn out, Democrats are poised to bounce back strong.

But our prospects raise two big questions. First, is embracing a message that virulently opposes President Trump's agenda sufficient to propel us forward *even after Trump is no longer on the ballot?* Second, even if that *is* a winning campaign strategy right now, what do we intend to do in office once we're back in power?

These two questions, while separate, are indelibly intertwined. If the American people react to Donald Trump's presidency with even a fraction of the disgust and anger the two of us feel, he's almost sure to be a one-term president. But if we intend to sustain a Democratic governing majority over the long term, we'll need an agenda (and an accompanying narrative) that stands on its own. Without a compelling message, we won't be able to hold on to the power that the public's revulsion to Trump may help us win. Then we'll be back at square one.

From where we sit, we don't believe that Democrats have yet begun to grapple in earnest with this quandary. In our zeal to castigate President Trump time and time again, we've failed to come to terms with the fact that, in recent elections, our ideas haven't resonated with vast segments of the American electorate. If more people were invested in our incumbent agenda—if they liked our existing ideas—Trump wouldn't have been remotely competitive in 2016. We should have trounced the Republicans in the 2016 presidential election, but depending how you think about it, we essentially came out at the losing end of a tie.

Don't get us wrong: we believe Democrats have plenty of good ideas—many of which would surely improve hardworking families' lives. But we also think that certain elements of our governing philosophy are well past stale. So, in the pages that follow, we'll introduce a new platform, what we like to call an "Opportunity

Agenda" for "Opportunity Democrats." Our aim is to help steer the Democratic Party back to power in a way that sets us up for long-term success.

Let's begin by facing the music. Whether or not they represent good policy ideas, there's nothing "new" in proposals to guarantee Medicare for All, or to raise the minimum wage, or to provide more generous family leave to new parents. The electorate has heard our candidates hawk this stuff for decades. President Trump's incompetence may be his undoing. But on a substantive level, Democrats today are still selling the same fundamental agenda we had on offer in 2016, even if some of the ideas are a bit more strident. We can't stress this enough: *that is a problem.*

What are we supposed to do to turn things in a new direction? Admit the truth: we need to refresh our agenda. Some will claim that the 2018 midterms proved that the old stuff is good enough—that we should just stay the course. But that's simply wrong. Democrats swept control of the House in 2018 primarily because voters were disgusted with President Trump. We didn't generate the landslide so much as we benefited from the GOP's implosion. To make a basketball analogy, we didn't steal the ball or block a shot and run a fast break. We simply caught the rebound.

Not that there's anything wrong with that—per se. By some measure, that's how opposition parties always find their way back to power. But Democrats will never make long-term reforms if our success depends on the GOP's failure. We need an affirmative strategy that establishes a majority, regardless of what the GOP is saying. We need a slate of fresh, new ideas that, on its own, convinces a majority of voters to support our candidates for office. If Democrats are going to get beyond "catching the rebound," we believe we've got to take the party in an entirely different direction.

THE LOST NARRATIVE

This book began as a collaborative project between two people who, on paper, appear to have very little in common. One of us is a New Yorker—the other's from the Midwest. One of us is a businessman, and the other has spent the last decade as a big city mayor. One of us is the spitting image of Denzel Washington—the other is not. And while we're both young, one is nearly a quarter century older than the other. (We won't say which.)

For all our differences, we share one central conviction: we believe the Democratic Party is due for a major disruption. It's not that we think the party should abandon its goals—we still want to help hardworking families achieve the American Dream. But we're both convinced that, to get our country pointed in the right direction again, Democrats need to rethink our approach.

Here's our *opportunity*. Millions of Americans—most Democrats, lots of independents, and even some Republicans—could be convinced to join a broad coalition if someone painted them a compelling picture of the way forward. Unfortunately, after decades listening to our tired messaging, whole swaths of America have pigeonholed the Democratic Party as so obsessed with growing government that we've lost sight of the greater good.

Our stale ideas are particularly inept for economic growth. Two things about the American job market are crystal clear. First, technology and globalization have left many hardworking people feeling exceptionally vulnerable. Breadwinners today hope to maintain the American Dream for the next generation—to ensure their children and grandchildren have it a bit better. But they fear that they'll hand off a world in which future generations aren't even able to sustain today's lifestyle. Remarkably enough, even during periods of low unemployment, many Americans are concerned about the prospect of *downward* mobility. At the same time, we know that prior to the COVID-19 outbreak, employers struggled to fill open positions—members of the workforce simply don't have the skills they require. In other words, amid a glut of demand, the workforce still fears being left behind.

Something has gone dreadfully wrong. Even after the economy recovers from the pandemic, it's likely many people will still fear they won't have the skills needed for the jobs that emerge.

Have Democrats offered any breakthrough ideas to help equip a vulnerable workforce for the jobs of tomorrow? Not that we've heard. Even if we *do* have good ideas, we've failed to message them so voters understand what we want to accomplish. We're too hung up on our old agenda. We're too accustomed to preaching the old "big government" gospel.

Does America have the capacity to resolve the mismatch? Unquestionably. If our universities, colleges, and community colleges establish programs to retrain Americans stuck in (soon-to-be) obsolete professions, we could boost millions into higher-paying, more productive jobs. But they aren't moving fast enough to meet the evolving demands of the country's businesses. *That's* the sort of problem our agenda needs to address *head on*.

Take one specific illustration: the president of the City University of New York's (CUNY) LaGuardia Community College recently revealed that she had invested more than two years—thousands of dollars' worth of staff time—procuring a single piece of software. The purchase had to win approval from one layer of bureaucracy...then the next. From the college's own faculty. From CUNY. From the State Department of Education.[1] Rather than focus on improving education, they were compelled to navigate a series of bloated bureaucracies.

For Democrats, that anecdote is a political disaster; it burnishes the public's sense that the very institution we tend to champion—government—is hopelessly inept. Our failure to bear down on this is both a substantive and reputational disaster. Even if Democrats champion education reform, we're held responsible for nurturing these unwieldy bureaucracies that prevent students from getting the training they need. We need an agenda that demonstrates that we're going to solve this kind of real-world problem. And we need voters to hear us make that argument time and time again.

Now, Democrats can go on talking about the issues that have long been at the top of their agenda—many have real merit. But the sort of red tape entangling LaGuardia Community College is rampant all across the country. Voters know that America's "systems" aren't working for them—higher education, health care, infrastructure, or criminal justice. And for many Americans, bureaucratic bungling has a larger impact on life than any single issue that's made its way into the Democratic bailiwick; it frames their view of government writ large. As a party, we haven't convinced the public that we're capable of fixing the underlying problems. We're not even telling voters that fixing these problems is at the top of our agenda. Is it any wonder they're not enamored with us?

Red tape isn't the sole issue holding us back. But we do believe that it's indicative of a larger problem. The incumbent Democratic agenda fails to address the challenges facing middle- and working-class families *from their perspective*. We too often endorse government-only solutions when their experience is that the private sector also has a role to play. We need to center our ideas on something else altogether: opportunity. And rather than remain caught in an ideologically driven approach, we need simply to present ideas that will solve the problems that voters grapple with in their everyday lives.

AN AGENDA *FOR YOU*

Here's the fundamental problem: rather than thinking comprehensively about how the world has changed since, say, LBJ crafted the Great Society in the 1960s, Democrats campaign and govern today in a defensive crouch. Our ideas center on preserving (and sometimes expanding) old, big government programs. Too frequently, that prevents us from speaking about the reality that defines middle- and working-class life in twenty-first century America.

Republicans have largely managed to avoid this problem because they offer a simpler, evergreen message. As Ronald Reagan famously said in his 1981 inaugural address, "Government is not the solution to our problem, government IS the problem." Whether true or not (and to be clear, it's not), Reagan's point resonated then with anyone who was frustrated with government bureaucracy. He offered a way of thinking about the world that was borne out in voters' everyday experiences—and, in many ways, still is.

Much as we Democrats focus our rhetoric on economic inequality and social injustice, our underlying governing agenda revolves around prescribing more government. Here's the dispiriting reality: too many Americans would rather stand behind a person like Donald Trump than embrace the standard bearer for the old Democratic agenda. They don't think our ideas are on point. And they aren't convinced by our messaging.

Take an idea that quickly became a cause célèbre during the Democratic presidential primary. "Medicare for All" is the latest in a long line of ideas to expand health coverage to the uninsured. It would undoubtedly be a boon for those who live in fear of medical bankruptcy. But what strategists frequently fail to ask—particularly in the wake of President Obama's misguided promise that "If you like your insurance, you can keep it"—is what, if anything, single-payer health care would do for the vast majority of Americans who already have insurance. And frankly, even if Medicare for All *would* benefit those who are already covered, we need to ask: Is that how voters *perceive* it?

Here's how Democrats need to think moving forward: Take any policy proposal—Medicare for All, free college, what have you—and consider whether it would make sense to tack the words "for you" to the end. Would the idea make sense for the broad majority of the American population?

Take the minimum wage, which is all too often the centerpiece of any Democratic candidate's economic agenda. From a purely economic point of view, raising the minimum wage often makes sense. Beyond benefiting those at the bottom of the wage scale, additional earned income provides working-class families with more spending money. Consumer spending drives growth. Someone nearer the bottom of the income ladder is more likely to return that money to the domestic economy than squirrel it away.

But raising the minimum wage is not an economic strategy that speaks to the whole of (what needs to become) the Democratic Party's national constituency. People making 150 percent of the minimum wage rarely think that they're going to be helped when government compels their employers to pay lower-wage workers more. The same thing applies to voters more firmly ensconced in the middle class. And the hard political truth is that explaining what we'll do for someone else simply isn't a winning strategy in a country where so many voters—many of whom make more than the minimum wage—feel so beleaguered.

In other words, as much as raising the minimum wage may spark broad-based growth, the accompanying message doesn't resonate with portions of the population, *and that's exactly what the Democratic agenda needs to do.* Voters who have acquired many of the basic trappings of the American Dream—a job with a living wage, a slate of decent benefits, a way to care for their children when they're at work—*also* want to know: What will the Democratic Party's ideas do *for me*? How will the Democratic Party's agenda expand opportunity *for me*?

We need to provide them with compelling answers.

BLINDED BY THE SWIRL

This all points to a confounding question: Why haven't Democrats produced a governing agenda and rhetoric that could appeal to voters outside our base? The answer is simple enough: we're so caught up in the political swirl that we've lost sight of what really matters. The back-and-forth on social media and cable news has distracted us from focusing on the topics middle-class voters discuss around the dining room table. That needs to change.

Here's the alternative: rather than trying to reply tit for tat to every GOP provocation, let's overwhelm the Republicans with better ideas. Let's compile a series of proposals better attuned to what ordinary working- and middle-class citizens *want* government to do. And then let's market those ideas in savvy ways that ensure they resonate with the very voters who were conned into voting for Trump in 2016.

Why have so many Democrats glommed onto Medicare for All? For a whole variety of reasons. First, the incumbent system isn't working as it should. America spends much more than most other advanced industrial countries delivering health care, even as a greater percentage of our citizens continue to trudge along without insurance. And the extra money we invest isn't even rewarding us with better outcomes. As the AARP recently reported, "The U.S. ranked last in life expectancy among developed nations through 2015 and is the only one of 18 countries with an average life span less than 80 years."[2]

But here's what gets lost in the Democratic Party's exclusive focus on expanding coverage: rising costs and middling care affect nearly everyone—including the vast majority of families with private insurance. Think about how you might see the health care debate if you had a sick family member *and* your family already had insurance. How would providing coverage to additional patients affect people who already wait for months to get a doctor's appointment? Perhaps you would still think those people deserved insurance—but you'd likely worry about the implications *for your* family.

It would be one thing if the American public had widespread faith in government to do a better job than the private sector on any given task. But they don't. Think what that means: the most talked-about Democratic idea in the health care arena offers very little benefit to those who already have coverage—and may even seem like a step in the wrong direction.

We don't mean to suggest Medicare for All can't work. In fact, we don't address the challenge of health care in the pages that follow; by now, most voters know that the Democratic Party is bent on expanding coverage (even if we don't always agree on how to get there). We're simply leaning on this example to make a point: making Medicare for All the centerpiece of the Democratic Party's health care policy explicitly tells voters that we're more interested in growing government than we are in solving for cost, which is the most pressing challenge for most middle- and working-class families. Democrats need to advocate relentlessly for solutions that both improve the lives of people without health insurance *and* reduce costs and improve care for those who already have coverage. And we need to adopt that same substantive approach to every issue.

AN OPPORTUNITY AGENDA

When President Obama tapped Anthony Foxx to be secretary of transportation in 2013, the Charlotte, North Carolina, mayor faced an entirely new kind of professional challenge. Mayors, as one of us can attest personally, have their hands in everything—they have direct knowledge of all the systems in their communities. How the highways work. How the transit system works. How the schools work. On and on.

Federal secretaries of transportation, by contrast, are much more removed. They make decisions that have vast implications for the country, but they can rarely anticipate how their decisions will reverberate outside the realm of roads and rails. The federal government funds projects and then lets the implications ripple out as they may.

In 2015, Foxx decided to change that. Rather than simply allot money project by project or formula by formula, he set a portion of the Department of Transportation's budget aside to create the "Smart City" challenge. Designing the program to resemble the Obama administration's "Race to the Top" education initiative, the secretary threw down the gauntlet: beyond the impact on transportation, applicants would have to propose how the transportation department's grant would be used to solve a non-transportation-related problem.

Columbus, Ohio, the city that ultimately won the competition, used its $40 million award to begin remaking its transit system, connecting neighborhoods with particularly high infant mortality rates to business corridors desperate to hire new talent.[3] But Foxx's initiative had impacts well beyond Ohio.

One of us, Mayor James, used the Smart City grant competition to get Kansas City thinking creatively about how to tap information and advanced technology to reduce traffic, build successful public-private partnerships, enhance mobility, reduce carbon emissions, curtail sprawl, and improve accessibility. His administration engaged with community members and local entrepreneurs to put an application together, establishing relationships that were destined to benefit the region whether or not they prevailed in securing the grant.[4] Kansas City received $500,000 as a semifinalist and used that money to invest in a powerful digital analysis platform capable of processing data from sensors placed throughout the region.

Why is the Smart City story so important? Because it illustrates the only true path back to an enduring Democratic majority: bringing a wide range of voices to the table. Thinking beyond individual programmatic imperatives. Taking the world as it is, thinking what might be done to improve it, and then asking not just bureaucrats but players in the public sector, in civil society, and private citizens to join in crafting the solution. If Democrats engage every public policy challenge with the same approach—and convince voters that *this* is our new governing philosophy—we will be much closer to building a lasting majority.

Think of how that would change our politics. Instead of letting Republicans define Democrats as the party of big government, we would be equipped to convince Americans that we were more directly focused on solving problems *for you*, no matter whether those solutions involved the government, business, or some combination.

None of the big problems facing America are going to be solved by the private sector alone. Nor will government magically save the day. But if we align citizens, businesses, academics, and policymakers, none of the big challenges America faces are too overwhelming to tackle. We just need to convince voters that we're committed to asking the right questions.

BEYOND THE REBOUND

A bold new Opportunity Agenda championed by a new generation of Opportunity Democrats isn't just a strategy to beat Trump in 2020. It represents an antidote to the demagoguery that's replaced thoughtful political debate. Bold new ideas will do more than simply achieve the results Democrats aim to deliver. They will allow us to move beyond our impulse to push back on President Trump when he gets out of line.

Take, as an example, the challenge of immigration—an issue that may have been, more than any other, responsible for Trump's successful campaign for the White House in 2016. Here's the truth: immigration is not the reason that the industrial heartland has faced new economic headwinds, or that manufacturing jobs have moved overseas, or that the American Dream seems so elusive to millions of Americans in the working and middle classes. Immigrants add vitality to communities with their ideas and hard work, and they pay much more into government coffers than they draw down. But let's not kid ourselves. No one denies that millions of people who never received explicit permission to be in the United

States are, in fact, living and working here. And while some say they live "in the shadows," the truth is that most interact with the rest of society in the normal course of everyday life.

We can argue about whether they're good or bad for America—we happen to think that they're a boon to our economy and enrich our social fabric. But even if every undocumented worker was beneficial to American society, their collective presence within our borders sends an unmistakable message: Washington has lost control. The US government doesn't have a handle on who comes into the United States and who is able to stay.

So what does that mean politically? No matter whether you believe 1) that everyone here without valid paperwork should be rounded up and deported, 2) that everyone here today should be offered amnesty, or 3) that there's a more thoughtful middle ground, no one can really dispute that the immigration system is broken. It is a clear and present example of government falling down on the job.

Donald Trump might have exploited underlying racism and xenophobia when discussing immigration on the campaign trail in 2016. But his message resonated because, even among those who might take a different view of immigrants themselves, Trump's visceral anger reflected their frustration with a brain-dead government. Don't America's citizens have a right to expect government to be able to keep track of who's in the country? Shouldn't the American people expect a minimal level of competence from their government?

Conventional wisdom argues that Trump is somehow a unique figure in American politics—that his "populist" message came out of nowhere. But in reality, he's just a more profane embodiment of the same core message that propelled Ronald Reagan into the

White House nearly four decades ago. The best antidote to Trump's politics isn't to castigate him over and over. It's to offer an opportunity-centered policy agenda that makes more sense to a deeply frustrated electorate—and market it with real savvy.

So here's what this book proposes: rather than simply excoriate Republicans, troll @realDonaldTrump, and beat the drum for big government solutions, Democrats should walk along a different path. We believe our Opportunity Agenda should be tethered to the values that have long fueled our movement—namely, the desire to help people who need a hand up. Enough of yesterday's ideas. Let's abandon our dependence on the rebound. We have an opportunity today to plot a new way forward that will work *for you*. Let's get to work.

CHAPTER 1

THE MOST IMPORTANT YEARS OF OUR LIVES

Crawfordsville, Indiana, is about as red as red America gets. Located roughly an hour west of Indianapolis, it serves as the seat of Montgomery County, where, in 2016, voters favored Donald Trump over Hillary Clinton by more than fifty points.[1] Nine in ten residents are white. The town boasts a plant that melts down recycled steel. A local printing plant has been open since 1921.[2] Absent George Washington coming back to life and running for president as an Opportunity Democrat, our party's nominee is unlikely to win an outright majority in Crawfordsville in 2020. But even if we can't win outright, we can do a lot better if we address the issues that people in Crawfordsville are facing head on. Don't forget: Barack Obama won Indiana as recently as 2008.

But how? The challenge for Opportunity Democrats is to identify which ideas will resonate, to peer directly into the experience of middle- and working-class families and ask what we can do specifically *for them*. To those who view Indiana (and places like it) as nothing more than "flyover country," Crawfordsville probably appears like little more than a town of "rednecks" who couch latent racism in tropes about economic insecurity. But red America isn't all one and the same, and Crawfordsville faces a challenge that afflicts many cosmopolitan communities as well: a glaring lack of affordable childcare for working families. That dearth of good options is undermining the local economy.

Here's something that may shock many in blue America: Crawfordsville was *not* struggling with unemployment before the COVID-19 pandemic hit. It hadn't for years. In fact, the unemployment rate in the state of Indiana bested national unemployment figures.[3] That's why the foremost complaint among Crawfordsville's employers was so remarkable. The cap on growth wasn't *opportunity*. It was *labor*. Earth to Democrats: the issue in Montgomery County, Indiana, was that *employers couldn't find people to hire*.

To be fair, it's not that every able-bodied person in Crawfordsville has found a professional opportunity to their liking—they haven't. But in all too many cases, people who *could* be working can't afford to fill those jobs because they can't find affordable, dependable, high-quality, year-round childcare. One recent study found that Montgomery County passed up nearly $5 million in economic activity because parents were absent from their shifts to take care of their kids. Five million is a bundle anywhere—but it goes particularly far in the rural Midwest. The resulting loss of economic activity drains public coffers, forcing local residents to hand more of their own income over to government tax collectors. In Montgomery County, an additional $5 million in economic activity would provide local government with more than $800,000 in revenue—money that middle-class families might not then have to fork over.[4]

The same basic problem is true all over the state of Indiana. One study recently estimated that only 12 percent of families across the state have opportunities to enroll their children in pre-K or licensed childcare.[5] And that reality recently left Crawfordsville's Republican mayor, Todd Barton, searching for answers. "We're starting to sort out some solutions on a local level for our workforce challenges," Barton said. "When we've tried to identify the root causes, it's very clear that childcare rises to the top of that list and that it keeps a lot of people out of the workforce."[6]

Crawfordsville's story shines a spotlight on something that is true in pockets all over the country. People in the prime of their lives— most of them women in their twenties, thirties, and forties—are boxed out of the professional American workforce simply because they're raising children. That reality robs many would-be workers of the opportunity to earn a good living. It deprives employers of productive employees. It can also prevent children from taking advantage of the kinds of social and educational advantages many can glean from preschool and childcare—a fact that will subsequently hamper the nation's economic growth when they mature into working-age adults.

It's a bad deal all around in both red *and* blue America. And when something is a bad deal all around, it's an opportunity for Democrats to craft solutions that can help us build a sustainable national majority. We need to get moving.

To do that, however, we need to answer a straightforward question: How do Democrats plan to provide childcare *for you*? What are we going to do to make sure that *you* can hold down a job during the years when you're raising your kids? Opportunity Democrats can't let this become a program that inadvertently opens the door for parents to shirk their parenting responsibilities in service of, say, watching television. Quite the opposite; we need to frame this idea as an explicit investment in growing America's economy both now and in the future. To harvest the vast untapped potential of America's workforce, we need to expand the availability of childcare *for you*. And that's exactly what we propose to do.

THE OTHER DROPOUT SCOURGE

It was no surprise that Chrissy Houlahan joined the military. Service was, in her own words, "the family business." Houlahan's father and grandfather had both been career naval officers, but because she'd long dreamed of becoming an astronaut, she decided to focus on the Air Force. As an undergrad at Stanford, she signed up for ROTC; after receiving her commission, she was assigned to Hanscom Air Force Base in Massachusetts.

Chrissy married Bart, her college sweetheart; they met in their freshman dorm. Having children changed everything for Chrissy and Bart (as it does for all new parents)—but they both intended to continue working. At the time, they were living off base because base housing was limited, as was childcare. While the military was a relatively welcoming space for families, most of the programs were designed with a "traditional" household in mind. Reality hit—and it hit hard. "Maternity leave was six weeks long, but you needed to wait six months to be able to have your child in base childcare," Houlahan explained. "I think that back then, there was sort of this assumption that the active duty member would be a man and the trailing spouse would be able to accommodate the six months until base childcare would be available." Childcare on the open economy in Boston was simply unaffordable on her salary. She did what millions of Americans have been forced to do in similar circumstance: she quit, transitioning from active to reserve service, and went on to pursue a graduate degree, even bringing her infant daughter with her to class at MIT.[7]

Viewed from the outside, the Houlahans' story seems utterly outrageous. America needs people like Chrissy keeping us safe. But the military essentially rejected the active service of a Stanford-educated, third-generation soldier because it provided no way for her to affordably care for her children. Of course, this narrative isn't all that uncommon: so many American families find themselves in similar situations, having to navigate simultaneously building families and careers. And without either party focusing sufficiently on the problem, that reality exists throughout the economy and across the country. Now, to hear the Pentagon brass talk, the military is more family-friendly than most employers.[8] (Small businesses often struggle to cover even the most minor accommodations.) So, if this dilemma befell a promising, well-educated Air Force recruit, think of what's going on in the private sector. How many talented potential employees are sitting at home for lack of other options? How many businesses are forced to settle for less-talented employees—or are unable to fill important positions altogether? How many points come off the nation's GDP each year as a result? Chrissy and Bart Houlahan's story is a tale of America kicking dust into its own economic engine. Millions of Americans are being forced to leave their family income behind—but Democrats have yet to explain how to fix that problem *for them.*

Fortunately, the Houlahans' story didn't end there. After leaving active service, Chrissy went on to find childcare, earn her master's degree from MIT, and lead a very successful, decades-long career in the private sector. She and Bart settled outside Philadelphia. Eventually, she enrolled in Teach for America and became a chemistry teacher in North Philadelphia. But her penchant for public service was never extinguished, and in 2018, she was elected to Congress as a Democrat from Pennsylvania's Sixth Congressional District. Because she's never forgotten the hard choice to leave active military duty, she's made access to childcare (and the effect its absence has on the economy) a big part of her agenda in Washington—in her first term, Chrissy led the passage of paid parental leave for all federal workers.

Make no mistake: there's nothing wrong with staying home to raise your young children, either as a mom *or* as a dad. But in America today, too many people are forced to step away from their careers (or forgo professional opportunities altogether) because they have no realistic alternative. That's not good for parents like Congresswoman Houlahan. It's not good for employers like the Air Force. It's not good for our economy. And, as research reveals, it's not good for children either—or, to put it in economic terms, the workforce of tomorrow.

Here's an issue just calling out for a solution—a challenge faced by families in both red *and* blue America. It's time for Opportunity Democrats to get in the game. It's time for us to begin targeting our agenda *and* our rhetoric to families falling behind because they don't have a safe place to leave their kids when they're on the job. Those can be our voters—and they should be.

WORKPLACE GHOSTS

Here's the current reality: in the United States, three things happen almost inevitably when a new baby is born. First, government support disappears almost entirely. Yes, federal initiatives like the Women, Infants, and Children (WIC) program try to ensure that very young poor kids are given some basic nutrition. Partnerships like Children's Health Insurance Program (CHIP) provide a modicum of health care coverage. But, in many cases, up until a child is enrolled in kindergarten (or in pre-K where it's offered), families are otherwise on their own. That's a stark contrast from what government provides from years five through adolescence, when public schools partner with American parents to mold young people into fully fledged members of society. During those *later* years, parents may worry about the safety and quality of their child's public school and education, but they know at a minimum that there's somewhere to send their kids during the workday.

The second thing that happens is a direct result of the first: absent any other reasonable way to care for their kids, parents— most often mothers—either drop out of the professional workforce or scale way back. More than two in five mothers with young children recently reported that "being a parent made it harder for them to advance in their career"—a figure that compares to one in five for fathers.[9] As a result, the American economy is being robbed of a whole cohort's potential productivity, and those families are being robbed of that income.

The third thing that happens is too often ignored. Because *someone* has to pay the rent, parents unable to stay home are often compelled to leave their children in unregulated, unqualified, informal childcare networks. They depend on relatives, neighbors, friends, or perhaps the elderly couple around the corner. Sometimes these arrangements work out well—but in many cases, they don't. Rather than trying to keep up with a hyperactive toddler, Grandma just plops the kid in front of a television. The neighbor leaves a young kid to play by herself, entirely unattended. In too many cases, a child's day is spent being warehoused, rather than being nurtured.

Beyond the human element, the economic implications are severe. Many of these "workplace ghosts" might otherwise become a firm's most productive employees. Because many are young, they don't command the sorts of salaries that their more seasoned colleagues might receive. But because they're (more frequently) right out of school, they're often in better touch with the technology and challenges of the moment. Think about it. Without adequate childcare and preschool, our system essentially bars parents from the professional workplace. And it's not just that they lose their present-day income. Those (mostly) mothers who are forced (or choose to) stay home later face the additional uphill burden of these extended leaves from the professional workforce. They've forgone the promotions they might otherwise have earned. And they surrendered the years of accrued Social Security benefits that they would have otherwise been able to claim.

This gaping problem emerged by accident. During the Industrial Era, it emerged under the guise of what we now call "sexism." Women were *expected* to stay home—and if they *did* join the professional workforce, it was in one of a limited range of professions. Too often, they were only offered opportunities to become secretaries, nurses, or schoolteachers.

Over the past several decades, two things have changed. First, while glass ceilings still exist, a much larger share of the nation's working-age women are joining the workforce across a much wider range of professions. According to the Department of Labor, between 1948 and 1999, the percentage of working-age women in the workforce grew from 32.7 to 60 percent (though it has since fallen back to 56.8 percent).[10] Public expectations have changed as well. Today, Americans *presume* that most adults, regardless of gender, will enter the professional workforce, regardless of whether they are married. When the early welfare program Aid to Families with Dependent Children was created in 1935, it was designed to provide enough support to allow white widowed mothers to avoid entering the professional workforce. But that old-fashioned standard came back to bite single women, who were attacked as recently as the 1990s for being "welfare queens" even as they raised their children in or near poverty.

Remarkably, neither party has made addressing this challenge—updating public policy to allow parents to stay in the professional workforce—a central part of their agenda. We can only guess why Republicans won't touch it. While they're often too cowardly to say it outright, they're still bought in to the obsolete idea that women should stay home. Democrats, we suspect, haven't focused on it for a different reason altogether: as a party, we're too focused on older students and older people. We talk about free college and prescription drug prices all the time. While those are important issues that speak to demographics that, in some cases, are most likely to cast ballots in any given election, they shouldn't be considered to the exclusion of one that's so challenging for so many young families. Opportunity Democrats need to make sure that voters understand that our approach to the early years of every family's life builds an infrastructure of supports explicitly *for them*.

HOW KIDS LEARN

Love them or hate them, "screens" have become an inescapable part of American life—particularly for children. A generation ago, many parents were already worried that their kids were watching too much television. But now we've entered a whole new world. With phones and tablets, screen time is mobile—and it's ubiquitous.

What exactly does this have to do with early childhood education and day care? On the surface, very little. But it points to something powerful: not every childhood experience sets kids up with an equal chance to succeed in life, let alone achieve their American Dream. What happens during the early years affects how successful you are decades down the line. What too many of America's leaders fail to appreciate is that voters understand that.

So what's the best way to raise a productive, happy, well-balanced adult? Parents have long debated whether young children are better served by staying home with a parent (or caretaker) or enrolling in a day care program. But the truth is that those two categories can't be compared one to one. Spending your early years with a loving, nurturing, attentive caregiver may provide a terrific springboard to lifelong success. But a childhood spent with harried parents who feel compelled to put you in front of an endless loop of cartoons is less likely to nurture the same sorts of life skills. On the other hand, some day care programs are better than others. The "best" scenario really depends on the individual child and the specific setting.

The real question is this: Beyond giving parents the bandwidth to thrive in their careers, what could we do to give them the confidence that their children are being molded into productive adults? The answer is exceptionally simple: ensure that the nation's childcare facilities are providing high-quality instruction.

Over the last several decades, researchers have come to understand that intellectual stimulation during a child's first years is a crucial determinant of their life trajectory.[11] It's in those early years that humans undergo 85 to 90 percent of their brain development.[12] In other words, infants and little kids need more than to be simply fed, clothed, and cleaned during their early years. Caregivers and parents need to help develop their minds. Parents are often amazed when, soon after birth, infants respond to an adult with an outstretched tongue by sticking their tongues out as well.[13] Our brains are programmed for social interaction. But though Democrats are inarguably the education party, we've largely failed to put early childhood development at the forefront of our agenda. That needs to change.

To be sure, parents don't need Big Brother to tell them how to raise their little ones. But too many adults aren't entirely sure how to equip their children for success. Some parenting skills can be taught. Go to your local bookstore, and you'll see reams of books designed to tutor parents on developing their children's minds. But not every mother or father has the time or inclination to read those books and absorb the underlying advice. To build the workforce of tomorrow, government should augment the love parents give their children with the sorts of tools more easily employed in a classroom-type setting.

Take all of these considerations together: the immediate impacts on parents forced to abandon their professions; the short-term impacts on businesses who lose valuable employees; the long-term implications for the workforce of tomorrow. Now imagine a world where childcare *wasn't* an issue—where parents could work for the entirety of their careers without being forced to drop out, however temporarily. People in their prime would be able to contribute more at work *and* at home.

That's not to say we should abandon the issues we've worked to champion for years. We should work to make college more accessible. We should address the dropout crisis among high school students. But for many families—particularly families with little kids—the government can do much more to help point the way to a better life. Nowhere in American life is the gap wider between what we *do* provide and what we *could* provide than in the first five years of any child's life; Democrats need to remind voters of that fact as often as they can. Which leaves us with just one question: how can Opportunity Democrats make childcare accessible for the families struggling to balance career and family?

START AT BIRTH

Every parent knows the feeling of panic mixed with joy and excitement when you bring that tiny bundle home for the first time. Most new mothers and fathers have spent years of their young lives anticipating that moment. They can't wait to get acquainted with the little person they've created from nothing. But almost every new parent soon realizes that, in many respects, they're in entirely over their heads. Nothing trains you to care for an infant or prepares you for the exhaustion and frustration of those first several months. And for that reason, from the moment we're put in charge of a little person's life, we worry incessantly that we're doing something wrong.

Recent research suggests that, despite the overwhelming sense that there must be a "right" way to parent, science actually doesn't teach us as much as we expect.[14] The choices moms and dads make about whether to nurse a baby or use formula don't have the outsized impacts many tend to believe. But certain interventions *can* change the trajectory of a child's life right from the beginning. It's enormously important, for example, to read, talk, and play with children when they're young. Similarly, overly harsh punishments for bad behavior can stunt a child's emotional development.[15] In these cases, family behavior can ripple out across a person's life. And in too many circumstances, parents have no idea.

More than a decade ago, a parent and educator named Geoffrey Canada noticed that many families living in Harlem, the historically African American neighborhood of New York City, weren't aware of how their parenting styles might affect their children. So he decided to establish a program called the Harlem Children's Zone Baby College—a nine-week curriculum designed to provide parents and caregivers with important information on a whole variety of subjects. The course included information on everything from how to enroll in Head Start to how to prevent asthma.[16] Eager to spread the gospel, Canada didn't wait for parents to enroll in the program—he hired recruiters to find and enroll them. Lo and behold, the program has proven a huge success.[17]

That being said, the fact that Harlem needed a program like Baby College is telling. And it's not just parents in blue America that can benefit from programs like Baby College—it's true in red America as well. The actress Jennifer Garner, who often jokes that she grew up in West Virginia "one generation and one holler removed from poverty," has become a champion of Save the Children, a nearly century-old organization that provides home visits to the parents of kids up to three years old, and a ten-day program to help older kids get ready for kindergarten.[18] Testifying before Congress on the state of children in rural America, Garner made the crucial point: "A child…who is not spoken to, who is not read to, or touched within the first five years of his or her life will not fully recover."[19] But how many parents all over America really know that?

The point is not *where* the programs are run or who pays for them, public or private. The point is that programs like Baby College and Save the Children should be available *everywhere* in America—in communities rich and poor, blue and red. And those programs shouldn't be there simply because they're a helpful service—they should be there because we know these early investments will eventually pay dividends. Tired of paying taxes for prisons? Frustrated that your business struggles to find high-quality employees? In response, Opportunity Democrats need to advocate for investing more in children at an early age. Programs like these can help ensure that fewer Americans drop out of high school and miss out on college, that more reach their fullest potential once they join the professional workforce.

Moreover, the support should continue with home visits throughout the course of a child's young life. Programs like Parents as Teachers, Healthy Families America, and the Nurse-Family Partnership were once the norm all across America. They sent trained professionals to visit parents and serve as trusted resources for mothers and fathers otherwise prone to isolation. To this day, a gentle nudge from someone who understands the travails of parenthood can make all the difference.[20] But these programs are now frequently starved for funding—and in too many communities, they're simply not available.

As Opportunity Democrats, we should take a page from the private sector's playbook to get programs like this up and running *everywhere*. Enfamil and Similac sometimes give free samples of formula to parents in the hospital, keenly aware that if the baby responds well to any given formula, the parents are likely to stick with that brand until the child is weaned onto solid food.[21] We should take the same approach to quality infant care—ensuring that parents are given opportunities to get "hooked" before they've brought their child home.

PAID FAMILY LEAVE

The second part of any thoughtful strategy to improve the way America handles the first five years of life should center on the first several weeks. Decades ago, Republicans liked to run campaigns on what they called "family values," a not-so-subtle shot at the core Democratic principle that a woman's body is hers and hers alone. Today, however, it's a real contradiction to be "pro-family" and also contend that parents should be forced to go back to work right after a child is born. Nevertheless, by opposing paid family leave, that's what Republicans are doing. They've made life impossible primarily for the nation's mothers. Democrats should hammer that point over and over. Our agenda promises real benefits *for you*.

The Family and Medical Leave Act, signed in 1993, guarantees employees of companies with more than fifty employees the opportunity to take a few *unpaid* weeks off without losing their jobs.[22] But given the fact that the cost of living has outpaced wage growth over the last several decades, is it any wonder why many families can't hack the prospect of giving up their income after a baby arrives? Too often, during the early weeks of a child's life—the very period when a baby should be bonding with its parents and a mother should be recovering from the physical trauma of childbirth—moms and dads are distracted by the question of whether they'll be able to make rent. As a result, parents are forced to run prematurely back to work. In the interim, they transfer that stress onto their vulnerable and sensitive infants—which can stunt a child's emotional growth.[23]

When one of us became the mayor of Kansas City, he established the Women's Empowerment Initiative as one part of a comprehensive effort to get the city's government running better. The conversations Mayor James had with municipal employees quickly highlighted the fact that many saw *paid* leave as a critical challenge. They weren't making exorbitant salaries. They'd each chosen to sacrifice the higher incomes available in the private sector for the stability of a career in public service. But across the board, they were frustrated that, without necessarily intending it, city policy treated them like miscreants when they had children. City workers had never been granted any paid leave, a convention that compelled contemporary workers to use their accrued sick time and vacation instead. As a result, when they returned, many were left without the flexibility to even take their children to the pediatrician.

At the time, Mayor James was engaged in a citywide program to determine residents' most pressing concerns. It quickly became clear that the challenges associated with early childhood were a huge issue for the private sector as well. Men and women *both* want the opportunity to get settled over the first several weeks of a baby's life; the question was whether the city's approach to municipal workers could have a ripple effect on private businesses throughout the region. So the mayor took a chance. In 2016, he created a program making Kansas City one of the first cities in the nation to guarantee six to eight weeks of fully paid parental leave for all city employees. "Implementing parental leave was a way we could start walking the talk," said Dr. Julie Holland, education adviser to the mayor. "We're the tenth largest employer in this city. The message to businesses was: if we can do it, you can do it."[24]

When pressed, not every private employer was enthusiastic. Many feared that the shift would drain too much from their company's bottom line. During the time a new parent is at home, employers have to pay their salaries and cover their benefits. But City Hall itself found that the costs of providing leave were fairly minimal—departments were able to handle the absence without much trouble, and the new policy sparked waves of gratitude that lasted well past the moment the parents returned to work. Many private-sector businesses have since found the same. And that's the point. While Democrats advocating for paid leave often talk about the benefit to the families, they fail to note that it's actually good for the economy and for the businesses that provide the benefit. Paid leave is a strategy designed not only to be good for families, but also to rev up the American economy in the short and long term.

Certain exceptions need to be made, if only because in small businesses where margins are thin, this sort of allowance can be too significant a drag on balance sheets. But in larger businesses that *can* afford to provide this sort of paid leave, it's a no-brainer: good for the child, good for the parents, and, in cases where employee appreciation sparks deeper loyalty, good for the business. If America is going to adapt to a reality where both parents in most families are expected to work in a professional setting, Democrats need to forcefully advocate for paid parental leave. It's the sort of benefit that parents will remember for the rest of their lives.

FILL THE WORD GAP

Efforts to use the first years of life to shape a productive future workforce shouldn't end when parents go back to work. If Opportunity Democrats are to convince parents that we're putting their child's economic potential at the center of our agenda, we need to demonstrate how we'll help each child's brain develop. How and when a parent stimulates a child's mind during those early years impacts how they will think for the rest of their lives—it may even affect their cognitive architecture. And while the government is never going to take the place of a primary caregiver—we don't live in a "nanny state"—there is certainly more public officials can do to encourage parents to prepare their kids for success.

In recent years, science has shed new light on one magically simple way parents can help their children: talk to them. Even before they can speak themselves, adults should do more than make goo-goo noises, tempting as that "baby talk" may be. Certain skills—hearing various words, deciphering what they might mean, and then figuring out how they fit in context—develop very early in life, well before children learn to talk on their own. So speaking to children when they're very young can give them a huge advantage as they mature. A talented or hardworking kid can overcome a word deficit later in life—but too few parents realize that simply voicing additional words in their babies' presence can have a real impact.

Several years ago, New York mayor Michael Bloomberg caught wind of this research, noting in particular that children growing up in low-income neighborhoods suffered disproportionately from a lack of word exposure; they were being exposed to a full 73 percent fewer words than their peers in wealthier homes. The result was that these children accrued, on average, a thirty *million* word deficit over the course of their first three years. Bloomberg was determined to do something to close the gap. His philanthropic foundation issued a challenge, hoping to encourage a city to tackle the issue head on.

Not long thereafter, Bloomberg Philanthropies selected Providence, Rhode Island, to receive a $5 million grant to set up a comprehensive intervention.[25] Under the auspices of a program that became known as "Providence Talks," families with small children, most of whom lived in low-income neighborhoods, were supplied with age-appropriate books and LENA Digital Language Processors to monitor the number of different words each participant heard during any given period of time.[26] Data was then taken off the LENAs, analyzed, and used to deploy home visitors to help parents develop strategies to talk to their children more frequently.[27] As of 2019, nearly two thousand children had participated, and roughly three in every five graduates were being exposed to additional words in their home.[28] That represented remarkable progress closing the gap.

The Providence Talks model is proliferating, in large part at the behest of the Bloomberg Philanthropies' "What Works Cities" initiative, which announced in September 2019 that it would support efforts to replicate the program in five additional American municipalities around the country. And the same impulse is inspiring other places more organically. Kansas City is among the cities that have also begun experimenting with LENA Digital Language Processors, deploying teams of home visitors to coach parents on how to weave more words and language into their young children's lives.[29] The results are incomplete to date—but the stories are very promising. If these sorts of home-based interventions become the norm in

American society, children are almost sure to arrive in public school ready to learn. And if Americans understand that the Democratic agenda is geared toward providing a better life specifically for *their* children, swing voters will be much more likely to vote blue.

CHILDCARE *FOR YOU*

Ultimately, of course, no matter what else is done to expand family leave or improve the support we give to the parents of small children, there's no way around the most fundamental issue. If Opportunity Democrats want to give parents of young children the ability to maintain their professional careers with only brief interruption, we need to provide them with more opportunities to enroll their kids in high-quality day care, preschool, *and* pre-K. Many conservatives ignore this issue because they still believe that a woman's place is at home. Democrats, on the other hand, overlook the challenge because, on the whole, we're too focused on high school and college. It's time for us to pivot—every family in America needs a place to send young children during the hours that parents are working.

The existing reality is stark. In Kansas City, enrolling a child in a full-day, quality pre-K program generally costs about $12,000 a year. The median family income is about $52,000 a year.[30] No matter how you cut those numbers, the conclusion is unavoidable: if a parent is paying for housing, groceries, transportation, and other necessities, a $52,000 budget can't cover a $12,000 line item on pre-K. While parents shouldn't be given license to abandon their basic responsibilities, America needs to do better.

Twenty-six-year-old mother of two Bria Anderson was recently caught in this very bind. As an Iowa State undergrad, she initially managed to afford childcare with help of public assistance. While living with her mother, the local social services agency considered her "homeless," and she was able to use the cash assistance to cover the $400 monthly tuition charged by the early childhood program at the St. Mark Center in Kansas City. Unfortunately, once she got her $26,000/year job with the federal government—a job that, after taxes, paid her about $16,000/year—she no longer qualified for public assistance. It was only because her mother agreed to help cover the tuition cost that Bria was able to keep her daughter Brielle in childcare. In Bria's experience, many a mother (and rarely a father) faces similar circumstances.[31] And those circumstances are resolved too frequently by a parent choosing to set their career aside.

What if Opportunity Democrats launched a nationwide effort for affordable, accessible, and year-round day care facilities? Several years ago, a survey revealed that 40 percent of Kansas City was a quality childcare desert—parents living in those neighborhoods had no high-quality facility to leave their kids at when they were at work. Would-be childcare providers are out there—but many report that, under present conditions, it's simply not feasible to open a new program. Childcare facilities are expensive to build because they demand shorter toilets, extra safeguards, and impenetrable fences, among other special features. Insurance premiums are often astronomical. And for what parents can afford to pay, staff salaries are often close to minimum wage, forcing providers to deal with rapid staff turnover.

So what should we do? First, and most important, we should make supporting childcare expansion a touchstone of our economic growth agenda. Precedents exist. More than a half century ago,

LBJ's Great Society created the Head Start program for children a year out from kindergarten. In some places, Head Start now provides *two* years of care. The vast majority of states already provide *some* funding for pre-K.[32] And cities ranging from Kansas City to Denver to Seattle to San Antonio to Cincinnati have developed programs to expand access to early childhood education and childcare. Despite those efforts, too many parents continue to suffer in the absence of a quality childcare facility. Solutions should be tailored to each individual childcare challenge, but the Democratic message should be the same: We are the party intent on helping the parents of young children *stay at work*. We are committed to expand America's access to childcare *for you*.

New York is pointing the way forward on this front. Mayor Bill de Blasio's signature effort to stand up a universal pre-K program in the five boroughs launched in 2014. Since then, enrollment has grown nearly three times over. Remarkably, using widely accepted standards of quality (Were the sandboxes clean? Were the kids able to sit and concentrate?), evaluators determined that New York City had improved the aggregate *quality* of the programs even while expanding the citywide *head count*.[33] But the next step is proving trickier—and Opportunity Democrats nationwide should take note, because the Big Apple's experience may be instructive. De Blasio is trying to expand the pre-K program to three-year-olds, providing families with two years' worth of childcare before their children are enrolled in a bona fide kindergarten. But Department of Education officials have struggled to find sufficient space.[34] Throughout the country, we need to crack this nut. If Democrats can provide the tools required to save parents from the nightmare of choosing between work and childcare, we'll have gone a long way in convincing the nation's electorate that we're working for them.

A SUBSTANTIAL RETURN ON INVESTMENT

How powerfully would a comprehensive strategy affect the American economy? The evidence is in—and the conclusions are almost irrefutable. A decade ago, the municipal government of Washington, DC, established a program providing tuition-free preschool to every three- and four-year-old living in the District of Columbia. In response, a full tenth of local mothers decided that, rather than pause their careers to stay home, they would instead remain in their jobs. As a result, the percentage of mothers working while raising young children rose from 56 percent to more than two in three.[35] Think of how much those women surely contributed to DC's economy by remaining in the professional workforce. DC's experience suggests that allowing parents to work fuels the economy—childcare pays dividends, almost literally.[36] Set the impact on the children aside—the conclusion is that free childcare is good for the economy.[37]

What's true in blue America is true in red America as well. According to one university study, Montgomery County, Indiana, loses $4.9 million per year due to childcare-related absenteeism—a figure that rises to $1.1 billion for the entire state and equates to more than $118 million in lost state tax revenue.[38] A similar study in Georgia found that the Peach State loses as much as $1.75 billion a year in economic activity for the same reason, and that more than 20 percent of parents in Georgia had left a job, quit school, or abandoned a job training program because of childcare complications.[39] A study in Minnesota found much the same thing.[40]

If the statistics are sobering, the anecdotes from parents who can't afford to remain in the professional workforce are heartrending. Rebecca Linke had a part-time job in the suburbs of Boston and was raising three children with her husband when she got a dream job offer. As she described it: "In my preferred field. At an organization with a strong mission that I support. Amazing benefits and, with personal days, more than four weeks of vacation every year. A bit farther away from home than I would have liked, especially in Boston traffic, but that was something I could have lived with." Excitedly, she accepted the offer and quickly called to place her youngest child into preschool. That's when she got the childcare bill. After an agonizing weekend with her husband going over their family budget, Linke decided to reverse course. Her family couldn't afford to let her pursue her professional dreams. Heartbroken, she canceled the additional preschool and called back to decline the job.[41] Her career would have to wait.

And, over the long run, her earning potential would suffer. As PBS reported not long ago:

> A 26-year-old woman who's making $50,000 when she takes three years off of work to attend to a child would leave not just $150,000 in lost wages on the table, but an additional $200,000 in lost wage growth—the cumulative effect of time off on future earnings—and some $165,000 in lost retirement assets and benefits. (The $165,000 includes missed 401K contributions and their assumed growth as well as reduced Social Security benefits.) That's a potential life income loss of $514,073—assuming taking Social Security at age 65 and investing 5 percent of income in a 401K with an employer match.[42]

That's a lot of lost income, a lot of lost productivity, and a lot of revenue that taxpayers then have to cover by other means. So, when Republicans dismiss childcare subsidies by arguing that they're too expensive, Democrats should counter that the cost of *not* providing those subsidies is an even bigger burden.

THE SOCIAL RETURN ON INVESTMENT

The benefits extend beyond the economy. Consider what's happened in Kansas City. Nearly a half century ago, two nuns came up with an ambitious plan to help poor children—they would establish a nonprofit devoted exclusively to that mission. Sister Berta Sailer and Sister Corita Bussanmas of the Sisters of Charity of the Blessed Virgin Mary began by developing programs for children living on the city's streets. They managed to get control of an abandoned gas station, converted it into a play space, and opened their doors, often to overwhelming demand. To finance the center's programming, they asked for charitable donations, and the people of Kansas City responded. The nuns' efforts, which became known as Operation Breakthrough, grew from there.

Over the years, Operation Breakthrough has evolved and expanded. The organization recently conducted a capital campaign that raised a whopping $17 million. And Sister Berta and Sister Corita have put those dollars to good use. In September of 2018, the charity opened a huge new facility to welcome children from throughout the Kansas City region.[43, 44] Seen today, it's a miracle to behold. Visitors on any given afternoon will see hundreds of small children—many of them African American children from poor families—engaging with skilled teachers on how not only to build bridges with blocks but also how to deal with interpersonal conflict. For children and adults alike, the most important skill is to know how to work productively with people who have different points of view.

What's less evident but undeniably true is how those skills transform children's lives. Every small child benefits from the sort of care, love, attention, and structure that's characteristic of any high-quality childcare or preschool facility—but particularly children born to parents struggling with poverty, addiction, mental illness, or other disadvantages. If you participate in an early childhood education program, you're 15 percent less likely to have to repeat a grade. You're more likely to graduate from college and find a job. You're more likely to own your home as an adult. You're less likely to become an addict or suffer from chronic disease.[45] One study suggests that the return on educational programs for four-year-olds is sixteen dollars for every one dollar invested.[46]

Moreover, the returns aren't just long term, and they don't accrue *only* for the children who enroll. San Antonio, Texas, recently completed a study of local children and found that students who had attended public preschool programs were two-thirds less likely to be placed in expensive special education programs. They were much less likely to be absent from school years down the line, a figure that impacts the amount of formula-based state aid flowing into the city's local public schools. In fact, by reducing truancy, San Antonio's school budget accrued an extra $23 million in state aid.[47]

And the medium-term benefits are impressive as well. Research indicates that students who attend high-quality preschool programs are more likely to excel when they get to kindergarten, which makes it more likely that they'll be reading at grade level by the end of third grade.[48] If a child is *not* reading at grade level by the end of third grade, he or she is four times more likely to drop out of high school, and the unemployment rate for young adults who drop out of high school is nearly double that of their peers who graduate.[49, 50] Even if high-quality childcare or pre-K isn't the single most important factor in determining lifelong success—and it may well be—it *can* change an individual's trajectory. And that's a big deal.

Here's perhaps the most eye-opening facet: one study of children in Chicago found that for every dollar invested in preschool education, the government saved seven dollars in the costs of criminal activity.[51] Not every study reflects the same results, but even if the Chicago study had double or tripled in the estimated impact, the up-front costs would be well-worth the long-term return.[52]

A WINNING POLITICAL ISSUE

Nearly half a century ago, President Richard Nixon argued against federal support for childcare facilities because, in his view, such a policy would "commit the vast moral authority of the National Government to the side of communal approaches to child rearing over against the family-centered approach."[53] The world has changed—societal attitudes have shifted to welcome women into the professional workforce—yet Nixon's approach to childcare still prevails. That marks an opportunity for Democrats. Here is an arena where we can offer benefits that will both deliver dividends for our society *and* provide a service explicitly for families.

Opportunity Democrats should highlight this crucial partisan distinction. We need to make voters understand we believe that everyone, regardless of their gender, should have the opportunity to strike the right balance for their family between home and work. We believe that the central question isn't how Americans can return to a bygone era—it's how we can make the best of our new reality for every single family. Given the powerful evidence of what a full-scale expansion of childcare and preschool would do for America, it's hard to understand how anyone could oppose it. *This is an idea explicitly designed not only to promote family values, but to drive economic dynamism.*

Some portion of the electorate doesn't want to hear any of that. But most Americans, including many who live in the exurban communities that voted for Donald Trump in 2016, want opportunities to embrace tomorrow's opportunities, and they know that the burden of finding childcare is real and almost invariably oppressive. Our approach to the first five years of life could win over portions of the electorate that would provide the margin Democrats need to sustain their majorities. It deserves to be at the center of our policy agenda and political approach in the years to come.

CHAPTER 2
A SECOND REVOLUTION IN AMERICAN EDUCATION

In the nineteenth century, a period when American commerce centered on agriculture, one-room schoolhouses prevailed across much of the country. With student bodies that could range across a dozen years, children received what most of us today would consider only the most rudimentary education. But by some measure, that was fine. In most cases, the *real* learning was done back at home. To survive, younger generations needed to know how to work the fields, care for the animals, and maintain a home. Those sorts of skills weren't built by reading textbooks or perfecting handwriting—they were taught directly by their parents.

Then, at the dawn of the Industrial Age and through the course of the twentieth century, the American economy needed workers to have a different sort of education. A new wave of jobs demanded something beyond the basic skills taught in the typical one-room schoolhouse. So a series of reformers began establishing the systems that are now in place. William James, Edward Thorndike, Marietta Johnson, and a host of others worked to build out a new paradigm of public education in which elementary schools and high schools would become the norm—and they succeeded. States, often through local officials, became responsible for providing citizens with the opportunity to earn a high school diploma. Big public institutions— the sort of high school depicted in 1978's *Grease*—became central to American life, replacing the one-room schoolhouse.

To be fair, one-room schoolhouses and big public high schools never represented the gamut of American education. Prestigious public universities have existed in some form throughout American history, some of them founded even before the Revolution. And we shouldn't overlook the ways major legislative shifts (e.g., the passage of the GI Bill) created and expanded various realms of education, like community colleges. But the basic narrative remains. Throughout the nation's history, educational institutions have been molded to align with the broader economy of each era. Nineteenth century schoolhouses produced students capable of thriving on the farm. Twentieth century high schools produced graduates prepared to secure good paying jobs. Unfortunately, the economy has turned again, from industry to information, and from the twentieth to the twenty-first centuries, but the nation's education system has yet to adapt.

A high school diploma today is now little more than a ticket to the minimum wage. During a period in which robots and artificial intelligence are poised to replace factory workers and truck drivers, the workforce needs more and better education. Employers are begging for change, all too frequently unable to recruit enough employees with the skills required for their businesses to grow. Here's the challenge: the nation's educational institutions need to begin serving up the workforce that the nation's businesses demand. Opportunity Democrats need to become the champions of whole-sale reform. We need to shape the nation's schools to either prepare kids to enter the workforce of today, or if they're not equipped to do that, to give them the foundation of knowledge required to succeed in college, community college, or at a trade school.

Americans know that too many of today's schools aren't up to the task of preparing future generations to claim the American Dream. And they have been calling for reform for decades, yet government hasn't delivered. In the early 1980s, the federal Department of Education published "A Nation at Risk," a report that infamously stated: "If an unfriendly foreign power had attempted to impose on America the mediocre educational performance that exists today, we might well have viewed it as an act of war."[1] Two generations later, the situation is nearly as dire. In 2016, roughly four in every five students entering the City University of New York required remedial education; they hadn't mastered skills they should have learned in high school. A year later, that number *appeared* to improve—fewer than two of three incoming students needed extra help. A closer look revealed the progress was due not to improved high schools, but to lowered standards: the university had dropped its trigonometry requirement.[2] And that's an apt metaphor. In American education, things get worse even when they appear to be getting better.

Years ago, the educational reformer Geoffrey Canada was speaking with Mayor James on the margins of an education summit. He offered up a bit of wisdom in the form of a math riddle: "Train A leaves Kansas City at 10:00 a.m. traveling at 90 mph and heading for Denver. Train B leaves Kansas City at 10:15 a.m. traveling at 90 mph and heading for Denver. When will Train B catch Train A?" The answer is: NEVER. You can't catch up moving at the same pace. And many of America's schools aren't even keeping pace, leaving successive generations to enter the workforce further and further behind. Schools are not solving the problems ordinary people face every day. And in an era of global competition, unless we speed the pace of reform, many American students will never be able to thrive.

If high schools were equipped to provide the nation's employers with the sorts of employees they need, everyone would benefit. But very little has changed from the era of Rydell High. It's not just that getting a high school degree is no longer sufficient for those looking to sustain a middle-class lifestyle. It's that the whole educational ecosystem—the institutions, teachers, and prospective employers that should guide the process—has yet to adapt to the changing nature of work. Democrats need to stop defending the status quo and begin demanding a system that empowers future generations to prosper in an increasingly competitive, information-based, global economy.

The public knows what's up—that's why faith in our education system has been in the gutter for decades. Roughly 50 percent of Americans had confidence in public schools in the mid-1980s—but that figure has fallen to barely more than one in three.[3] How do ordinary people experience the system's failure? They see that students, through no fault of their own, are being launched into careers holding diplomas that have little value for prospective employers. They hear about employers desperate to hire additional workers but unable to locate real talent. While that's a disaster for both the economy and the country as a whole, it marks an inflection point for Opportunity Democrats. If we can prove to voters that we have a workable plan to fix a failing educational ecosystem, we will not only have addressed a pressing national priority. We will have proven our value to the sorts of people who grudgingly voted for Donald Trump in 2016.

So how should Opportunity Democrats solve this problem? In the previous chapter, we focused on what we can do in the first five years to spark the economy and expand opportunities both for parents and, in the long run, their children. That's the foundation for success. But beginning in primary and secondary education, American schools need to do a much better job. If we're going to demonstrate to voters that we are best equipped to drive economic growth and broad-based prosperity in the decades to come, we need to offer a credible plan to turn around the nation's public schools. That begins by talking to parents in language they understand and trust.

Educators today are prone to throw out lots of jargon— STEAM education (science, technology, engineering, arts, and mathematics), "teaching to the test," "noncognitive skills," "rote memorization." But really, American educators should be focused on one primary goal: closing the so-called "skills gap." We need to uproot an outdated system and install a new paradigm that will give future generations the skills that they'll need to thrive in 2050. And here's the good news: *we can do that.* Opportunity Democrats simply need to convince the country that we have what it takes to get the job done.

THE SKILLS GAP

Let's begin by defining the problem we're trying to solve *for you*. Here's what we believe: first and foremost, the nation's education system should produce graduates that tomorrow's employers will want to hire. What does that mean, exactly? What skills will tomorrow's economy demand? We can't be sure—no one has a crystal ball. But we know enough to begin fixing the system now. And there's really no time to spare.

First, we know that machines are going to be employed for an increasing share of whatever can be automated—the sorts of jobs that were once found on assembly lines, at industrial mills, and deep within coal mines. While that may at first appear like a strike against adolescents who dream of becoming truck drivers (a profession automated vehicles may eventually render obsolete), the truth is that automation doesn't necessarily mean *less* work—it simply means *different* work. Employers won't need drivers, but they *will* need people to manage and program the trucks. And that's a simple example of how educational systems need to adjust: schools need to be sending students into the workforce prepared to program and maintain those trucks, rather than to drive them.

Opportunity Democrats need to focus on that good news—we need to paint a more explicit picture of how the economy is going to work *for you* if you work hard and get the education America *should* provide every citizen. For all the doom and gloom about the end of the American Dream, and even after the COVID-19 debacle, *there will be jobs.* Moreover, scores of other countries have already figured this out. The places where the robot-to-worker ratio is highest (namely Germany, Korea, and Singapore) have very low unemployment rates.[4] And that's for a simple reason: automation not only makes businesses more efficient and productive, but it also creates demand for *new human positions*.

Denmark's decision to train workers to handle 3-D technology helped propel Danish companies to worldwide leadership in hearing aids.[5] Canada's largest province, Ontario, provides low-skilled workers displaced by technology with as much as C$28,000 in training grants—and enrollees have their transportation and childcare subsidized through the program.[6] American communities should be doing the same—figuring out how demand is poised to evolve, and then supplying a workforce to meet it, with machine learning and artificial intelligence woven into the equation.

That means changing both the broader and narrower realms of education. From a macro perspective, we need to imbue tomorrow's students with what a World Bank study on the future of work explained are the keys to a successful twenty-first century career. "Three types of skills are increasingly important in labor markets: advanced cognitive skills such as complex problem-solving, socio-behavioral skills such as teamwork, and skill combinations that are predictive of adaptability such as reasoning and self-efficacy."[7] As we explored in the previous chapter, the foundation for acquiring these more universal capacities is laid in the early years, largely before any student enrolls in kindergarten. But public schools subsequently need to burnish those skills as children get older. In essence, the workplace of tomorrow is going to require people who can think—a change that's already fast upon us.

It's impossible to over-estimate how important these skills are for today's workers. One recent study found that the percentage of jobs in advanced economies that require "non-routine cognitive and socio-behavioral skills" has risen from 33 to 41 percent since 2001.[8] Can you think through an unexpected problem? Can you work with other people to solve it? If you were a line worker at the widget plant in 1955, you might not have needed to be able to do either of those things. But now, that's *exactly* what employers demand of the people they hire. And if you *don't* have that capacity, you're likely to remain a step behind.

But it's not just these broader skills that employers demand. America's schools need to do a better job equipping graduates with the specific skills that local employers are looking for. It's terrific to instill a love of learning in future generations—but employers want to hire people with very specific competencies. If Opportunity Democrats are going to convince voters to let us lead economically, we need to demonstrate that we're prepared to connect in-class instruction to the jobs students are likely to get when they emerge with their diploma. For example, if the local economy is largely fueled by bio-tech firms, local schools should be producing graduates with the ability to hit the ground running on their first day. If the local economy centers on machine learning, the same. If students understood that the work they do in class is a prerequisite for jobs that would earn them, say, six figures, they would be much more inclined to run through the tape of high school graduation. But as of today, that's simply not happening.

Finally, sometimes begrudgingly, educators are beginning to come around. Many (quite reasonably) fear that preemptively steering students away from college preparation may clip a student's wings. No one wants to deliver the deflating message to an adolescent that they're not equipped for the rigor of a college education, or that they shouldn't shoot to enter fields that require more advanced degrees.[9] But many of the job openings in America today don't require a college education—they *do*, however, require a certification beyond what students get either in a traditional high school or college. Moreover, a study out of Massachusetts found that vocational programs can combat the impulse to drop out of high school—they keep students in school. Knowing that you'll emerge from twelfth grade with a certificate that will enable you to jump right into a lucrative field incentivizes students to stick with their educational careers.[10]

School districts around the country are beginning to incorporate this new wisdom into the way they approach their mission. The Shelby County Schools that educate students from Memphis, Tennessee, once printed T-shirts emblazoned with the message "Every Child. Every Day. College Bound." More recently, however, administrators have dedicated $6.7 million to overhaul the district's job certification program, offering students opportunities to prepare more directly for fields that range from barbering and cosmetology to web design and criminal justice.[11] As a district spokeswoman explained, "We're going to have a career pathway for every child, no matter what that looks like."[12] That's exactly the right attitude.

All of this puts America's educational system at a pivotal intersection. If the United States was destined to face economic circumstances devoid of good jobs, we would need to take a certain political tack—perhaps we would be wise to consider guaranteeing every family some basic guaranteed income regardless of whether they worked. But that's explicitly *not* the reality we face. There *will* be jobs. There *will* be demand. We simply need an educational system that bridges the gap between the nation's workforce and the employers of tomorrow.

The business community is already on board—and for obvious reasons. One survey recently found that nearly three in five employers struggle to fill vacancies inside of three months.[13] And the growing failure of the labor market has had a direct effect on working- and middle-class prosperity. Between 2018 and 2030, the failure of schools to produce workers who *might* be hired by the financial and business services sectors is slated to cost the global economy more than $1.3 trillion, of which more than $430 billion will be lost in the United States alone. Technology, media, and telecommunications aren't far behind. But here's the kicker: America's manufacturing sector is *also* hungry for talent. An average of ten thousand baby boomers retire *every day*—a reality that will exist for the better part of the next two decades.[14]

Americans *know* that our educational system is failing. They don't have to be convinced with statistics—they see it in their everyday lives, both among those looking to hire new employees and those looking for jobs. If voters can feel in their bones that the nation's education system needs to be reimagined, Opportunity Democrats need to offer substantive ideas to turn things around. This is not a moment to offer piecemeal reforms. We need to come up with an alternative for those in school today and those who will enroll in public schools in the generations to come.

SCALING THE WALLS

You might presume that education reform is almost a gimme for Opportunity Democrats—the lowest of low-hanging policy fruit. But anyone who has dealt with American public education knows that even the smallest changes face stiff resistance. If, as we believe, the government has a role to play in improving people's lives, then preparing future generations for tomorrow's opportunities should top our broader agenda. But the record shows that, all too often, liberals are on the wrong side of education reform. The moment reformers suggest an aggressive change, Democrats too frequently morph into champions of the status quo. If Opportunity Democrats are going to pull the party out from under that reputation, we need to acknowledge why we so often choose the easy option rather than the right one.

Decades ago, government decided to offer educators a bargain of sorts: taxpayers would pay them a pittance of their worth (what, after all, is more important than teaching future generations how to think?) in return for job stability (read: tenure) and a schedule that *purports* to be more forgiving than that of other jobs. In reality, the bargain was never entirely on the up-and-up. Classroom hours may be short—but most teachers also spend hours preparing at home. And while salaries were never generous, they've become increasingly miserly. As the *Washington Post* found in a recent investigation,

> In the early 1990s, when today's veteran educators were starting out, public-school teachers and support staff pulled in above-average paychecks in 26 of the 42 states for which the Labor Department had comparable data. By 2017, their earnings topped the average in just one state, Rhode Island. Over that time, public-school teacher and staff earnings fell relative to the average worker in all 42 of those states.[15]

Today, many talented educators don't want the sort of deal older generations accepted—and it's no mystery why: millennials have been raised to believe they're liable to have four or five careers before they reach retirement age. They don't want to take a job whose benefits pay out only to those who stay locked in the same school district for decades on end.

Importantly, the actual job requirements have changed over the decades. Teachers today are asked to do much more than their counterparts two and three generations ago. They are required to impart a new bevy of real-world skills to their students. At the end of the year, tests reveal whether they've succeeded. Being a public-school teacher is about as stressful a job as you can find, yet on a salaried basis, teachers are still paid just a fraction of what they contribute.

In essence, what we have is a massive professional mismatch. We treat teachers as though they're little more than old-style manual laborers. At the same time, we expect them to be true experts, shaping some of the most complicated and (as parents, we can say this) perplexing people on earth: children. The results are broadly predictable. Teachers often feel frustrated and unappreciated. Members of the community feel angry and disappointed. Most important, students come away undereducated. Everyone loses.

For Opportunity Democrats, this represents a chance to stand at the forefront of a movement for more comprehensive change—a grand bargain that would serve everyone better than the *status quo*. We believe it's high time for America to begin treating teachers like the professionals they are. In the end, if educators are going to be held responsible for helping to raise the nation's children—and, make no mistake, that's what they're doing day-in and day-out in the classroom—they need to be given enough tether to get the job done as they think best. They need both more autonomy *and* more training. They need both to be more empowered *and* to be more flexible. They aren't workers at a mill simply trading shifts. They are shaping minds and, in many cases, preparing the nation's future. As highly trained experts, they should be empowered to sink or swim on their own, and they should be paid commensurately. At the same time, they should not be able to hide behind work rules and red tape when they fail to perform.

For years, reformers looking to make big improvements have treated teachers not as partners, but as enemies. They vilified teachers' unions and complained about tenure. That has been a mistake—a self-defeating strategy. In reality, teachers aren't the root of the problem so much as they're a crucial part of any solution. We need to offer these men and women the respect they're due and the resources (including training and mentorship) required to ensure they succeed. That's a difficult balance to strike. Reformers can't expect the latitude to impose solutions from the outside. At the same time, union officials can't reject proposed improvements and changes out of hand, lest they end up defending incompetence beyond reason. Fortunately, examples have emerged to point reformers around the country in the right direction. And perhaps no example shines a light on how reformers and educators can work productively together better than Camden, New Jersey.

In 2013, after years of failed efforts to turn Camden's schools around, state officials took control from local education officials. They appointed a thirty-two-year-old Iranian refugee and former Goldman Sachs executive, Paymon Rouhanifard, as the district superintendent. Many local residents worried that Rouhanifard's arrival in Camden would spark a cultural battle between reformers and entrenched interests. To keep that from happening, Rouhanifard went on a one-hundred-day listening tour, and then built a system that demanded more significant investments from the charter school companies he invited to assist in turning the city's schools around—rules that convinced many local residents that more was being put into the schools than the outsiders were taking out. As the *New York Times* reported, in the more than five years he spent in Camden, "Mr. Rouhanifard—almost universally 'Paymon' or 'Mr. Paymon' to residents here—has won support in traditional public schools, as well, managing transformation without the rancor that has frustrated change in other cities."

The results bore out the wisdom of his approach.[16] When Rouhanifard left in 2018, NJ.com reported: "As recently as 2014, before reform took hold, as few as 4 percent of kids were proficient in math—a number that has now more than tripled, citywide. And in one of the poorest cities in America, one charter-managed school is now matching the state's average scores in math."[17] POLITICO explained: "The district's graduation rate is up 17 percent, and the dropout rate has been cut in half, to 11 percent. Suspensions are down by more than 50 percent. State test scores, while still quite low, are rising steadily."[18] And despite holdouts in some corners of the local teachers' union, most people who relied on and cared about the city's schools were more hopeful and bought in following the transformation. Byron Dixon, the principal of one of the city's previously failing elementary schools, was enthusiastic about the training teachers were offered for the first time during Rouhanifard's tenure—a program run by the founders of the charter school company Uncommon. As he explained, "I'm upset we didn't have this years ago."[19]

Why haven't things changed in similar ways elsewhere? Because the stakeholders are locked into the existing system. Local administrators are handcuffed by state bureaucrats who dictate the local curriculum and define "success." School officials are often uninterested in outside experts telling them what to do. Older teachers, many represented by union leaders, are uninterested in changing a system right before their well-earned pensions kick in. And younger teachers worry about what they might lose if they give up the old bargain. In sum, everyone in an increasingly obsolete system feels at risk of becoming, well, obsolete. And as the pressure mounts to make more radical changes, the various stakeholders become more voraciously defensive of their own interests. For obvious reasons, Democrats rarely want to get caught in the middle.

That's almost to a tee what happened in Providence, Rhode Island. When Governor Gina Raimondo invited a team of researchers from Johns Hopkins University to study the state capital's school district in early 2019, the experts were so shocked by the level of despair and dysfunction that some were driven to tears. It wasn't just the physical state of disrepair—it was the sense that a core group of educators who wanted to do well for the children of Providence were ham-handed by the system in which they operated. The report was devastating:

> The Providence Public School District is overburdened with multiple, overlapping sources of governance and bureaucracy with no clear domains of authority and very little scope for transformative change…The resulting structures paralyze action, stifle innovation, and create dysfunction and inconsistency across the district. In the face of the current governance structure, stakeholders understandably expressed little to no hope for serious reform.[20]

Our party has become remarkably hesitant to propose the sort of comprehensive reforms that America's education system demands and that convincible voters desperately want. Some critics have argued we're too beholden to the teachers' unions—and it's true that teachers provide a reliably Democratic base of popular support.[21] But the short-term risks of offending a few union officials pale in comparison to the long-term danger of leaving the system to wallow in dysfunction. If Opportunity Democrats are going to win, we need to convince frustrated parents that we believe their kids' futures are worth the risks we face in any given election. We need to deliver an educational system worthy of our own children and grandchildren.

Fortunately, we don't need to remain mired in the old debates between unions and administrators forever. As the story of Camden's evolution proves, we know how to break our school institutions out of their twentieth century rut and give future generations the twenty-first century education they deserve. In some cases, we will need to confront some sacred cows—but in others, Democrats simply need to work toward reform in good faith. In the end, the politics of education need to be a strength for Democratic candidates for office. If we offer winning ideas and present them in ways that people can understand and appreciate, they will be.

IMMERSIVE LEARNING

Think back to your own experience in high school. Almost all of us can recall a class we were required to take for no justifiable reason. How many of us have ever used the algebra we were forced to master? How many of us still play the instrument we were compelled to practice every afternoon? How many of us have ever had occasion to cite *Fahrenheit 451* in an adult conversation? If students see the connection between what they're studying and the salaries they'll earn from learning a subject, they're liable to devour the material and stay engaged. But too often there's no clear payoff for the hours of toil it takes to earn a passing grade. Opportunity Democrats need to champion efforts to bridge that gap.

Let's take a step back. It's not that students shouldn't learn English, math, science, or any of the other core subjects. Those classes are crucial to the ability to think critically—a capacity that, as the World Bank's research has indicated, will prove even more crucial in the decades to come. The liberal arts are a key building block for a creative and productive life. Math is a crucial stepping stone for programmers. But taken on its own, the old curriculum no longer encompasses everything students need to learn to thrive in the twenty-first century's global economy. Beyond any of the basic classes that have long been taught in the nation's high schools, today's students need much more specific skills to succeed in the jobs that are being offered (*and will be offered*) by local employers. Schools should therefore be teaching those skills *before* kids receive their diplomas. And when local businesses run into resistance from champions of the status quo, Opportunity Democrats need to be the change agents who make sure that employers are getting the workforce they need.

That's exactly what happened in upstate New York's Fulton and Montgomery counties. Local business executives, frustrated that they couldn't find recruits ready to fill local job openings, decided to take a new tack. Rather than attempt to entice well-trained outsiders to move into the community, the Chamber of Commerce worked with state officials to set up a new school through a program called P-TECH, or Pathways through Technology Early College High School. The idea was simple: the businesses would directly determine the local curriculum, and the students who graduated would have first dibs on job openings at local companies.

The key for programs like P-TECH—programs which have a small foothold around the country, but which Opportunity Democrats should champion relentlessly nationwide—is that they are explicitly *immersive.* Kids aren't staring off into space during the various classes because, far from thinking "Oh, I'll never need to know this when I'm actually earning my own living," they know that exactly the opposite is true. *What they learn through hands-on programs like P-TECH will have a practical application down the road.* The skills they learn are almost guaranteed to win them a job.

That promise was a powerful draw for Nick Suits, a local teenager who chose to enroll in a P-TECH program rather than the more traditional school nearby, Canajoharie High. His parents hadn't gone to college, and Suits presumed he wouldn't either. "I had no idea what I wanted to do," Suits explained to a reporter for the *Albany Times-Union.* "P-TECH…gave me a lot of skills, not only the hands-on knowledge stuff to work, but the professionalism. That really helps." And the P-TECH experience provided two additional benefits. First, upon graduation, Suits was offered a job at the GlobalFoundries Fab 8 computer chip plant, a facility where he'd interned while still taking classes. Second, during the course of his high school career, he'd accrued enough credits to get him most the way toward earning an associate degree, the sort of certificate students get when completing community college.

Nick Suits chose to focus his immersive education on manufacturing, a subject that was advantageous in his region because local manufacturing companies were eager to hire new employees. But immersive programs like P-TECH need not focus exclusively on any one field. In communities flush with cybersecurity jobs, similar programs can be established in partnership with local tech firms.

In places with companies performing back-end financial support, the same. The two keys are tying the program to local needs and integrating the experience with the employers themselves.

Why hasn't this approach been deployed more comprehensively? In part, because Democrats haven't championed it sufficiently. Of the roughly twenty-six thousand secondary schools in America, fewer than one hundred have adopted P-TECH, meaning that the program has a great deal of room to grow.[22] And the point isn't simply to make schools conveyer belts into existing jobs—it's to encourage kids to get their diplomas. In New York State, 95 percent of the kids enrolled in a P-TECH program earn their degree, compared to 80 percent more generally. Moreover, the program's graduates come away, on average, with more than twenty credits toward their college or community college degree.[23]

In other cases, programs designed to solve for this very problem blur the lines between high school and college education. In 1907, Ranken Technical College was established in St. Louis by an Irish immigrant convinced that the traditional American approach to education wasn't working for many of the city's most promising young people. He believed that students should glean most of their knowledge not in classrooms, but on the job sites where they would eventually make their living. Today, in that same spirit, Ranken awards certificates in sixteen different areas. They welcome a diverse student body, a portion of whom are in their late teens and go to school during the day, and another set of whom are often older and take classes at night. Many of the certificate programs operate using an "eight in/eight out" approach, meaning that students spend two months in the classroom and then two months in the field. After two years, successful students have generally acquired enough credits to earn their associate degrees—and more important, many have the skills required to get a job in one of the industries hiring in and around St. Louis.

Bridgette Weams is typical of many Ranken graduates. The daughter of a single mother, she dropped out of high school before graduating. Her mom wanted her to reenroll and get her diploma—but Bridgette decided to enroll in Ranken's electrical tech program instead. In Weams's case, that turned out to be the right decision. Three months after her Ranken graduation, she had a job offer from Sargent & Lundy, a construction and engineering company, making an annual salary of $58,000. She took the job, moved to Chicago, began accruing experience and seniority, and eventually enrolled in a program to earn her bachelor's degree.[24] Weams may not be a beacon of the "traditional" path in American higher education—but she's nothing if not a success.

That's why, from a political perspective, programs like P-TECH and Ranken are so important. They represent an alternative to the tired messaging Democrats tend to engage in on the campaign trail. More money! More benefits for teachers! Higher taxes! More redistribution! Immersive programs unquestionably require additional resources—though the businesses who will hire the graduates are often willing to share the cost. But if Opportunity Democrats are going to convince voters that they're pursuing an agenda *for you*, we need to prove we're not out primarily to sweeten pensions or redistribute income so much as to prepare the next generation for the jobs of tomorrow.

LENGTHEN THE SCHOOL DAY AND YEAR

Immersive education won't be for every student—some kids will still go to more traditional high schools. For that reason, Opportunity Democrats need a plan for how to improve existing educational institutions as well. For years, reformers have championed "charter" schools based on their conviction that families living near failing public schools should be given a choice, and that competition between existing schools and new alternatives would force the older institutions to up their game. But for all the good they've done, charters aren't everywhere. Moreover, in a political environment where charters are often political lightning rods, we need to embrace other approaches as well.

One crucial problem facing many school districts—an issue that is often tied up in collective bargaining agreements—is the measly amount of time that American students spend in the classroom. Countries ranging from Australia to Finland to Korea send students to more school than the United States—and in some cases the gap is a matter of *years*.[25] It's time for Opportunity Democrats to ask: What would happen if we extended the period each day we use to educate students? How much more would kids learn if they spent the equivalent of several extra days each year with a teacher? The truth is that we can't yet know for sure. The results depend largely on the quality of the teacher and the staying power of the underlying instruction. But states are beginning to experiment with both targeted and more widespread efforts to extend student instruction time, and the early returns are extremely promising. Beyond improving outcomes for individual students, additional instruction provided in the months *between* school years has been proven to reduce the notorious "summer slide," where students lose unused skills.

Like on many education fronts, the state of Massachusetts has led the way. More than a decade ago, the Bay State decided to invest a portion of their state budget in augmenting the amount of time students spend in the classroom. More than 70 percent of that funding went to support the salaries of teachers spending more time with their students.[26] In quick succession, their investment paid off. Between 2006 and 2010, state math proficiency measures rose by 20 points. Maybe even more important, the positive impact was more dramatic in marginalized communities. In an era where poorer and minority students find it increasingly difficult to get a toehold in the job market, extending the school day helps close an educational gap that breeds inequality.[27]

Other states have taken the same tack. Between 2012 and 2014, Florida lawmakers decided to focus on correcting for lagging English proficiency in some of the Sunshine State's lowest-performing districts. So, Tallahassee imposed new mandates requiring three hundred schools to extend the length of their respective school days to provide extra instruction in reading. Like in Massachusetts, the results were impressive, with the average results jumping almost as much as if the school year had been extended by a full three months. And again, it was disproportionately beneficial for kids from the most disadvantaged backgrounds—namely those eligible for free or subsidized lunches, and those learning English as a second language.[28]

These early demonstrations point to something profound: it may be worth exploring whether extending the school day—providing more consecutive hours of instruction—could be more effective than spreading the instruction out over a longer period of time. The program in Florida cost about $800 per student, but the value (measured by traditional indicators) was well more than

$3,000, suggesting, according to at least one analysis, that students get more from extending the day than they do from reducing class sizes.[29] If Opportunity Democrats are going to demonstrate that they are effective stewards of the public purse, they need to prove that they're spending taxpayer dollars efficiently. Here is a clear opportunity to prove the value of reform.

Fortunately, the emerging movement for additional instruction hasn't stopped in Massachusetts and Florida. New Mexico, one of the nation's poorest states, largely assigns responsibility for school funding to the state government, rather than to localities. When Michelle Lujan Grisham, a dynamic, young, Latinx, Democratic member of Congress was elected as the state's governor, she made school improvement a top priority.[30] Grisham's initiative centered on two programs, the first of which provides funding to cover the salaries and expenses of teachers who agree to work an additional ten days each year. To date, those extra state dollars have been harnessed to deploy different approaches in different municipalities. In Los Alamos, administrators used the funding to plan ten special Saturday sessions centered on experiential learning for older students.[31] In Farmington, School Superintendent Eugene Schmidt planned a ten-day math boot camp for incoming high school freshmen, giving each student a jump start on the year's algebra curriculum.[32]

Secondly, Grisham expanded "K-5 Plus," a program designed specifically with the state's lowest-performing school districts in mind. It extends the school year for elementary school students by a full five weeks each year, which amounts to 150 additional days over the course of a student's primary school education. Again, the state funding is designed as a proverbial carrot: teachers who agree to participate are eligible for a 14 percent bump in their salaries.

Albuquerque jumped at the program, with sixty schools in the city adopting it almost from the get-go.[33]

Of course, as Grisham and other Democratic leaders around the country have understood, none of these improvements can be deployed without incurring a cost. Improvements to public education—particularly improvements that require additional instruction—require additional investments. If public officials are going to ask more of teachers, those teachers deserve to be compensated. An average of 87 percent of every additional dollar devoted to education goes to salaries and payroll. And like in every other profession, you largely get what you pay for.[34] When Santa Fe District Superintendent Veronica Garia was asked about the additional time teachers would have to spend to staff K-5 Plus, she explained: "They put their whole heart and soul into their work. When we ask, 'Would you like to work an additional 25 days,' many of them are saying that we need a break."[35]

Fortunately, these sorts of conflicts can be resolved with deals that benefit both students *and* teachers. After test scores revealed that the students in several schools in Wilmington, Delaware, were struggling, school administrators worked out an arrangement with the teachers' union that extended the school year by as many as twenty days. Teachers were enthusiastic because they got several concessions in return. To relieve teachers from having to keep watch outside the classroom, the district hired lunch and recess monitors, school resource officers, permanent substitutes, and crisis response teams. The teachers were given tuition reimbursement and one-time bonuses of $4,000 in return for a two-year commitment.[36]

A NEW COMMITMENT TO LIFELONG LEARNING

Lastly, Opportunity Democrats' agenda for improving American education can't be limited to primary and secondary schools. We also need to enhance institutions designed to educate those who never graduated from high school. Moreover, we need to develop new ways to help individuals stuck in obsolete careers jump into emerging fields (like coding) that offer more upward mobility. Already, a range of organizations around the country are experimenting with various models to accomplish that goal. We need to learn from their experience and bring their best practices to scale around the country.

Jukay Hsu's story offers a case in point. Born in Taiwan, Hsu's family immigrated to Queens, New York, when he was four. Always a strong student, he attended a "nerd camp" with Mark Zuckerberg when the two were high school students interested in computer coding; he then went on to enroll, like Zuckerberg, at Harvard. But upon college graduation, rather than take a job on Wall Street or an established business, Hsu decided to join the military—to serve the country that had accepted his family with open arms. His unit was eventually sent to Iraq.

Soldiers almost always find war to be a life-changing experience, and Hsu's military service proved to be no exception. Having borne witness to the lives of people caught amid horrific conflict in Tikrit, he developed a new appreciation for how disparities in circumstance (as opposed to innate capacity) shape each individual's lifelong trajectory. With those Tikritis in mind, upon his return to civilian life, he decided to devote his life to expanding economic opportunity. Abandoning a long-held plan to go to business school, he instead founded the nonprofit Coalition for Queens (C4Q, which has since rebranded itself as Pursuit), explicitly to help working-class New Yorkers acquire the skills necessary to land middle-class jobs in the tech industry.

Hsu's organization was different in that it not only taught enroll-ees the nuts and bolts of coding, but also a range of other nontech-nical skills crucial to succeeding in the twenty-first century's digital economy—skills often unfamiliar to immigrant kids and children raised on the margins of society. The program included instructions on how to write a résumé, how to behave in an interview, how to work on a team, and how to take responsibility for managing a project. In essence, Pursuit sought to marry the skills taught in coding boot camps with the norms that are passed along in more expensive, longer-term educational programs. He provided a short-cut for employers desperate to hire the talent they need to grow.

Pursuit has grown to be a major force in New York—and tech companies are taking notice. Uber worked with Pursuit's LevelUp program to create career pathways for drivers like Abdelwahab Oufkir to become full-time software engineers. Oufkir emigrated from Morocco and started a master's program in political science at Arkansas State University. He had planned to finance his edu-cation himself, but he couldn't find a job in Arkansas and was forced to drop out. So he moved to New York City, got married, had two children, and, after trying his hand at everything from slaughterhouse manager to Central Park tour guide, started driving for Uber to support his new family and mother-in-law.

After settling into his new role, Oufkir fulfilled his old dream and graduated from Queensborough Community College with an associate's degree in computer science—a credential he hoped would open the door to new opportunities. That provided him with a solid foundation in coding, but a two-year degree doesn't necessarily translate to employability in today's job market. It wasn't until he got an email from Uber with details on the LevelUp program that he was able to launch a career in tech. Following a successful, ten-month intensive fellowship with Pursuit, Oufkir was moved into a software development role with Uber Eats that pays $90,000 per year—nearly four times the amount he was pulling down as a driver. Everyone benefited: he began earning a higher salary, and Uber Eats had essentially recruited a reliable new employee.[37]

Pursuit is undeniably at the cutting edge—but even if its approach was scaled dramatically, we should be clear-eyed that organizations like Hsu's can't fill the vast need for professional education without allies in the public sector. Because the demand is so acute, America needs community colleges, traditional colleges, and universities to engage the lifelong learning challenge in much more robust ways. For years, the world of higher education has talked about changing their business model to include students in need of something other than a traditional associate or bachelor's degree—but in all too many cases, administrators haven't seen the job through. Opportunity Democrats need to demand a new approach, reorienting the world of higher education to fill the skills gap more proficiently for the workforce of tomorrow. And to begin, federal, state, and local governments should partner with the private sector to establish competitive grant programs for new innovative curricula. We should call the program "Degrees of Tomorrow."

Here's how the program would work: If a community college president met with local business leaders and discovered that local companies were looking to hire experts in, say, software engineering, or artificial intelligence, or health care informatics, or supply chain management, or whatever else, she would assign her faculty the task of designing a program explicitly to serve that discrete need. To cover the cost of that work, the government would establish an incentive-laden grant program encouraging university administrators both to nurture new programs and weed out those that were no longer helpful.

Even without government intervention, some schools around the country are already innovating along these lines. Syracuse University's Maxwell School, for example, developed the Veterans In Politics ("VIP") program explicitly to serve former members of the military interested in entering the world of public service. Believing that the program had real merit, J. P. Morgan offered to foot a great deal of the bill.[38] At the University of Memphis, the FedEx Institute of Technology worked with the software giant SAS to develop student expertise in data analytics and business intelligence. The courses are designed to prepare existing and potential employees to pass exams developed and curated by SAS itself, making the university a gateway into an established company.[39]

To this point, these programs remain the exceptions and not the rule—but that could, and should, change. In the end, the point isn't *how* we create an ecosystem capable of ushering the workforce of the twenty-first century from one career to the next, or even from gig to gig. The skills gap today is so wide—and the demand for employees with specialized skills so overwhelming—that we need to take an all-hands-on-deck approach. Opportunity Democrats need to show the way.

EDUCATION *FOR YOU*

In the end, there are really only two ways to look at the state of American education. On one level, it's a disaster. Our schools aren't producing the workforce America needs if we're going to forge ahead as the globe's leading economy. Upon graduation, students are being sent to compete in a global jobs market without the tools required for success. The incumbent system is allowing the "skills gap" to widen. It can feel as though the wheels are quickly coming off the bus. Fixing the status quo represents a real political opportunity. We know what to do simply by dint of the fact that progress is being made in communities across the United States and elsewhere around the world. The situation isn't hopeless because we know what we need to do to build a better tomorrow.

That's not to minimize how challenging building a new educational ecosystem will be. The progression from one-room schoolhouses to vast public high schools was long and bumpy, and this next evolution has come with its share of challenges. But if Opportunity Democrats are going to win over the sorts of constituents who have been tempted into voting for Donald Trump or who *did* vote for Donald Trump in 2016, they need to at least get caught trying to make education better in the United States.

The ideas presented in this chapter are not designed to offer a panacea. Moreover, we don't demonize anyone trying to improve education in America. But meaning well isn't good enough anymore, and voters know that. We need fundamental change. And Democrats, if they intend to win elections, need to prove that they are the leaders willing to see that change through.

CHAPTER 3

"FIX THE DAMN ROADS"

Much too often, by the time she arrived at work, Sylvia Campos was already frustrated, if not angry. Every day she'd leave her home, get in her Nissan Cube, turn the ignition, and head to her office. And without fail, she'd encounter a commute through Detroit that was nothing short of a nightmare. Michigan's decaying roads weren't just bumpy—they were downright dangerous. "Every time I'm on the freeways, I'm scared," she explained. "But you can't do nothing about it 'cause you've just got to take the hit. You can't go to the right and you can't get to the left because you're going to have an accident. It's terrible. They need to fix them."[1]

You would have thought that Campos's complaint, echoed across the country, would have prompted politicians to action. After all, millions upon millions of Americans drive on the nation's highways, enduring the indignity of the decaying roads day in and day out. Dilapidated roadways are a hair's breadth from being added to death and taxes as the only certainties in life. Nevertheless, candidates for office rarely put infrastructure atop their agenda. That is, until they do.

Luckily for Campos, in 2018, when a county prosecutor named Gretchen Whitmer was running for governor of Michigan—one of the states that voted by the tiniest of unexpected margins for Donald Trump two years prior—she leaned heavily into a promise to "fix the damn roads."[2] Perhaps because Campos's experience was so universal, because so many Michiganders were desperate for improvements to the state's roadways, Whitmer won.

Unfortunately, Whitmer's story remains an outlier. In the context of President Trump's tweets—not to mention the wide range of issues that tend to dominate state and local political campaigns— the state of the nation's roads, bridges, airports, power lines, schools, and water systems gets scant attention. Whitmer's victory points to why Democrats might want to consider shining a brighter spotlight on the nation's infrastructure. This is an issue that touches people where and how they live. If government leaders were to solve the problems, they would unquestionably improve people's lives in a way that they would notice on a daily basis. This *should* be a case where Democrats quickly take advantage of a powerful opportunity. But we need to approach the challenge in a smart way.

Why are so many Democrats remiss in shining a spotlight on infrastructure? In some cases, the problem is little more than a lack of imagination; in others, we suspect something else is going on. We believe Democratic candidates fear that mentioning the nation's rotting infrastructure will simply remind voters of their frustration with incompetent public bureaucracies. With faith in government so dreadfully low, many Americans don't think either party is capable of putting a dent in the problem. Moreover, at a moment when the federal deficit has surpassed the $1 trillion mark, an open-ended spigot of new spending is likely to become a political liability.[3] In other words, highlighting the government's failure to solve this problem just reminds voters of how frustrated they are with government itself. And by many estimates, that's bad for Democratic candidates.

We understand that political reality. After all, it's easy enough to complain incessantly that Republicans are standing in the way of progress. But we don't believe our party can afford to leave this challenge unaddressed. If Opportunity Democrats are going to win over skeptical voters, we need to offer them a narrative that does more than delineate how bad the nation's infrastructure is. We need to point them toward a believable way out of the mess. We need to convince voters that we have the capacity to get the job done *for you*.

Here's the root of our challenge: Opportunity Democrats need to distinguish their current approach to infrastructure from the tax-and-spend regime that's prevailed for decades. For some reason—mostly, in our opinion, due to intellectual laziness—discussions of our decaying roads and bridges almost always harken back to a tired ideological debate between less government and more. But that's not really what we're talking about anymore. Every consumer has faced a moment where they needed to choose between a high-quality product that worked and a low quality product that never would. Americans *want* world-class infrastructure—and they'd be willing to pay for it. But they're not convinced that *either* party is capable of delivering the systems that the nation demands. And that's the sale Opportunity Democrats need to make.

We don't need to convince anyone that infrastructure needs improving—voters of all stripes are well aware of the problem. We need to convince them that we're the ones capable of fixing this mess *for them*. They are not interested in hearing us opine on the problem. They can do without high-minded initiatives to study the possible solutions. Opportunity Democrats need to become, in the public's mind, the party of progress. We need to articulate a vision that points the way out of the darkness. And we believe we can do exactly that.

"WE'RE LOSING"

Think back to the 2016 campaign. Donald Trump may have *appeared* undisciplined on the campaign trail, spewing seemingly half-baked invectives to audiences around the country. He often went beyond the impolitic, infusing his remarks with racist, sexist, and otherwise offensive rhetoric. But at its core, his message was simple, powerful, and direct: "We're losing," he would explain. And, for many in both red and (formerly) blue America, that rang true.

Outside a few walled-off beacons of economic dynamism— places like Silicon Valley, New York City, the Research Triangle in North Carolina, and Austin—it seemed then (in a pre-COVID-19 world) like the wheels were already coming off the American economy. Even in places like Chicago and Kansas City, the gap between what Trump advisers like Stephen Miller would call "cosmopolitans" and nearly everyone else seemed massive—particularly to those who perceived themselves to be getting the short end of the stick.[4] And nowhere was that dichotomy in greater relief than the state of the nation's infrastructure.

Infrastructure is different from other issues because, while business executives regularly complain about the impact dilapidated roads have on their bottom line, voters rarely cite it among their most pressing concerns. Asked by a pollster, Americans tend to bring up the quality of their kids' education, the burden of rising health care costs, and the struggle to save for retirement. But even if it's not top of mind, infrastructure festers in everyone's collective conscience. When Americans are on their way to work or driving their kids to school, the view out the windshield perpetually reminds them of government incompetence. And here's what Democrats too frequently fail to grasp: that reality burnishes Donald Trump's central message.

It's actually worse than that; for all that progressives complain that the residents of red America let themselves be blindly convinced by Trump's lies, when it comes to infrastructure, the public's impressions largely line up with the reality. One recent report from the American Road and Transportation Building Association used Federal Highway Administration data to tally 47,000 "structurally deficient" bridges in the United States.[5] During a recent three-year period, more than four hundred American schools reported heightened levels of lead and copper in the local drinking water.[6] And nearly one in three homes in rural America lacks access to standard broadband today, compared to little more than one of fifty homes in the country's urban cores.[7]

But it's not just that so many bridges are rickety or that your grandmother's internet connection is spotty. "We're losing," as President Trump likes to say, because we're losing jobs. If you can't get from your home to your office reliably because traffic is terrible or the trains don't run on time, you know implicitly that you're not just losing time—the economy is losing money. You're not the *only* person who's going to be late for work—so are all the other people who depend on the same route. And data back that up. The American Society of Civil Engineers has calculated the cost of decaying infrastructure to the American economy will be $7 trillion by 2025.[8]

Our competitors are heading in the opposite direction. China is investing in the very sorts of systems—high-speed trains, deep sea ports, brand new airports—that now appear beyond America's grasp. That's what's so dispiriting. We sent Neil Armstrong to the moon largely as a reaction to the Soviet Union's triumph sending Sputnik into orbit around the Earth. In the 1980s and 1990s, Japan and Germany were bogeymen—their cars, their electronics, even their ways of organizing their economies were purportedly more sophisticated than ours. But in the public's mind today, China is now in another league altogether.[9] And while perception and reality are often different, in this case, the two are largely aligned.

The statistics are daunting. Not too long from now, China's air travel market will surpass the United States in volume. And while many major airports in the United States feel dingy, crowded, and otherwise outdated, the Chinese are opening an average of eight new airports a year, growing from 175 in total to 260 between 2010 and 2020. Between 2015 and 2030, the Chinese "upper middle class" is slated to grow from 10 to 35 percent of the overall population.[10] If these trends continue, America seems destined to lose its place atop the global pecking order. And people throughout the United States—particularly in middle America—know it.

And it's not just China. One recent survey found that the United States ranked only eleventh in infrastructure globally.[11]

By 2025, more than 63,000 of America's nearly 91,000 dams will be more than fifty years old.[12] It's an international embarrassment—but Americans of a certain age know it didn't *used* to be this way. We weren't *always* getting our hat handed to us by global competitors. When Nikita Khrushchev came face to face with Richard Nixon in the famous "kitchen debate" of 1959, Nixon could boast that the United States was way ahead of the curve.[13] The substance of that argument seems laughable now—and that simply burnishes the sense that America is losing.

The upshot of all this is that infrastructure, which *should* be a source of strength for Democrats, has become a liability—a proof point for the underlying argument Donald Trump made to voters convinced that Americans are perpetually getting a raw deal. The challenge for Opportunity Democrats isn't to convince voters that America should be investing more in the nation's road, bridges, schools, wires, and pipes—that's obvious. It isn't even that those investments would drive growth—on that front, people are already sold. The challenge for Opportunity Democrats is to demonstrate that we have a real plan for actually building the infrastructure. And that's a much taller order.

Fortunately, a prominent and proven solution already exists. We just need to explain how we'll bring it to scale and make sure that voters associate it with the Opportunity Democrat brand.

MORE *FOR YOUR* TAXPAYER DOLLAR

For years, residents of both Kansas City, Missouri, and Kansas City, Kansas, had little choice but to purchase their internet and cable service through Time Warner, the massive telecommunications company that owned and maintained the region's predominant cable network. As you might expect, general consumer satisfaction with Time Warner's service was middling at best. Subscribers frequently reported that the service was lousy, even while the premiums were expensive. The network's connection speeds weren't spectacular by any stretch. And you rarely heard about a customer service experience better than horrendous.

Then, in 2011, the region was presented with a rare opportunity. Google, flush with cash and thinking about how best to grow their business, issued a sort of upside-down "request for proposals." In the normal course of business, states and cities regularly ask private developers to propose solutions to various challenges. For example, developers might be asked to submit competing plans for what they would do to improve a derelict lot. In this case, by contrast, Google asked cities to apply to become among the first locales to benefit from "One Gigabit to the Home." As an experiment, in return for the opportunity to collect bits of data, Google would set up an entirely new municipal telecommunications network that would be much faster and more convenient—new wires, new connections, new capabilities, and a real alternative to the lousy service many Americans were getting from traditional telecommunications companies like Time Warner.[14, 15]

After a lengthy application process, Kansas City, Missouri, and Kansas City, Kansas, won the competition together. Many in the region were elated. But it wasn't so simple. Google wasn't just constructing a new building on a site they'd purchased using equipment they already controlled. They were going to have to build One Gigabit to the Home on top of the region's existing infrastructure—and they would need agreements with the bureaucracies that owned and controlled that infrastructure to complete the job.

Taken collectively, that represented a tall order. If Google was going to deploy fiber beneath city streets—all in service to improving the telecommunications network for residents and businesses—executives needed to forge agreements with municipal bureaucracies. If the company was going to put sensors on publicly owned poles, executives needed cooperation from the region's utilities, including Kansas City Power & Light and the Kansas City Board of Utilities. In short, to complete One Gigabit to the Home, Google was going to have to connect with a whole range of public agencies. And that meant the Silicon Valley behemoth, accustomed in many cases to working independently of public bureaucracies, was going to have to enter into a whole range of "public-private partnerships," or P3s. Truth be told, some of those public bureaucracies weren't entirely bought in to the challenge. They had fish to fry that, from their parochial perspectives, seemed more important than partnering with a deep-pocketed corporation looking to piggyback on their publicly owned assets.

Newly elected in 2011, Mayor James made clear upon his inauguration that any department reporting to him needed to ensure that the partnership would work. The upside for his constituents was simply too high for any bureaucracy to stand in the way. He was to make the balanced concessions required to get the program up and running: reducing the fees the city charged for Google to place equipment on the city-owned poles on various street corners, coordinating Google's plans to lay new fiber beneath downtown streets even as the city was building a new streetcar system at ground level. With mayoral leadership, the partnership took off. In an effort to encourage residents to switch from Time Warner to Google's new higher-speed network, Google created a kind of friendly competition, pitting various neighborhoods against one another. Those "fiberhoods" that reached threshold numbers of households that placed a ten-dollar deposit on signing up for the service jumped to the head of the line for installation.

The upside of the partnership wasn't just that residents were empowered to jettison Time Warner's lousy product and enjoy faster internet connections while surfing the web. One Gigabit to the Home enticed scores of other companies to come to Kansas City. Sprint came and created a free Wi-Fi network downtown using Google's new infrastructure, and then purchased laptops for many of the region's high school kids. A founder who grew up in next-door Kansas established EyeVerify, a company that built retina scanners and face-recognition technology, eventually sold to a Chinese conglomerate for $100 million.[16] One Gigabit to the Home made the whole region more attractive to the business community.

City Hall benefited as well. With the new infrastructure up and running, a company called Exact deployed experimental analytics to help the city predict where potholes were likely to emerge. Another company, Smart City Media, erected kiosks throughout the city that allowed people to do anything from making restaurant reservations to calling for an ambulance. And the data collected off those kiosks, initially deployed along the streetcar line, is now used to help companies make decisions about what residents want and need in any given corner of the city.

Could Kansas City have searched for another way to get One Gigabit to the Home-type infrastructure? In theory, yes. Perhaps, if the city had waited a bit longer, Time Warner would have erected the same sort of system on its own—and perhaps it would have done so without asking for the concessions Google demanded from various regional bureaucracies. But in all honesty, that wasn't realistic then, and it's less realistic now. Time Warner simply wasn't interested in making the investment.

In some cases, communities have sought to make improvements in their broadband networks without outside help from the private sector. But, as *BroadbandNow* has reported, often with support from legacy telecommunications companies, twenty-five states have either erected barriers to what some call "community broadband" or banned new networks altogether.[17,18] In many cases, however, that's entirely irrelevant. "Community broadband" isn't a realistic possibility. Local leaders don't have the expertise, resources, or capacity to set up an alternative to commercial networks. And most taxpayers will tell you that they have no real interest in government taking a larger role in domains that the private sector now controls—save for holding those private businesses accountable when they fail to provide good service.

One Gigabit to the Home worked in Kansas City because it was structured in the right way. It was a partnership. It wasn't entirely left to the private sector—much as that's what free market fundamentalists might have preferred. It wasn't owned wholesale by bureaucrats, as socialists might envision the future. By establishing a public-private partnership, Google and the region's public sector created the only realistic way to provide new infrastructure that both equitably served the public *and* sparked new economic growth. The only way forward centered on working hand-in-hand.

This is the approach Opportunity Democrats need to champion. Here's a way to get things done and to illustrate that our party isn't opposed to private-sector success. We want companies to make money—we simply believe that the profit motive tends to be balanced against social and economic justice. Businesses, after all, often elicit more trust from the public than government.[19] If companies are going to search for ways to build capital—and they *are*, because that's what they *do*—we shouldn't instinctively castigate their executives. Quite the opposite; we should work collaboratively to make sure their financial interests line up with the greater good, and then make sure they hold up their ends of the bargain.

For decades, Democrats have fought for greater public investments in assets like infrastructure—and that's fine. But in a world where the public isn't seeing much evidence of those investments bearing fruit—at a time when many voters feel as though their tax dollars are being gobbled up to no good effect—public-private partnerships offer a smarter path forward. The question now is whether we can make the necessary pivot. Can Opportunity Democrats entice the private sector to become partners more frequently in the campaign to restore America's infrastructure? We believe the answer needs to be: yes.

A NEW RELATIONSHIP

Let's set the table for a moment—or at least take a step back. It's not that business and government don't interact in the ordinary course. They engage all the time. Business leaders frequently complain about overregulation—and their complaints are frequently on point. Public officials often worry that businesses are leaving vulnerable communities behind—and too often, that accusation is rooted in truth. But the relationships forged between the public and private sectors encompass much more than regulation and free enterprise. Companies depend on government to provide a commercial landscape in which they can do business. Government often depends on business leaders to help boost local economies. Their success, in essence, is mutually intertwined.

Conservatives often like to claim that businesses always know best and that government invariably gets in the way. Progressives seem too frequently to take the opposite approach entirely. But the truth is that neither side has a monopoly on wisdom. So, the challenge isn't to give greater power to either business or to government—it's to align them in service to the greater good. That's what Opportunity Democrats need to do. We need to explain why getting the public and private sectors on the same page is the key to getting things done—and then we need to map out how we intend to accomplish that.

The good news is that if you look around the world, you can see lots of successful examples of P3s working to great effect. South Africa, for example, knew that it needed better commuter train service between Johannesburg and the surrounding cities ahead of the 2010 World Cup. The question was how to drive the project forward. The limits were clear. The private sector had no intention of building the train system on its own, because there was no way that service revenues would cover the costs of construction and maintenance. But the public sector had no expertise in building a new commuter rail service. To get the job done, they would have to work in partnership.

The deal they struck was, at root, fairly simple. The government promised to provide a deep fund of capital to the company selected to design, build, finance, maintain and run the "Gautrain" system—$3 billion for the construction, and then a healthy annual subsidy lasting through the period the company ran the service. In return, the private company that won the contract would have to raise additional money, but would see the upside of keeping costs down and completing the project on time. With only a handful of minor delays, that's exactly what happened. Phase one of the project was delivered three days ahead of schedule. And today, South Africa is considering how to expand the system using much the same breakdown of responsibilities.[20]

The current incarnation of public-private partnerships began in earnest in the United Kingdom more than a generation ago, but they've since begun to proliferate across the world.[21] Canada, for example, applied the P3 model for the first time in 1997 when building the Confederation Bridge between Prince Edward Island and the mainland of North America. The project was so successful that governments throughout the country began issuing regulations *requiring* government to see whether a P3 would work as a first option.[22]

What's the secret to success? As it turns out, there's no real magic to a successful P3—like any worthwhile partnership, the terms need to be negotiated between the parties, and the deal needs to work for both sides. In some cases, as with the Gautrain in South Africa, the cost of the underlying project is well beyond what the private sector can afford to cover, so taxpayers are forced to subsidize the capital costs. In other cases, however, cash-strapped governments can hand control of dilapidated but *potentially* money-making assets over to the private sector, getting an infusion of cash in exchange for the right to collect revenues down the line.

That's how the state of Maryland approached the challenge of preparing the Port of Baltimore to handle larger Panamax-sized ships: they handed operational control of the facility to Ports America and Highstar Capital, which handed the government a lump sum of $140 million, agreed to an annual fee, and promised to share in the profits they accrued while operating the port. The

State then used the money to invest in more traditional infrastructure around the state.[23]

Our point here isn't to suggest that the P3s are a panacea. Not every important piece of infrastructure can benefit from having a private-sector partner. And P3s aren't a magical fount of money. The public invariably ends up paying a fair share of the costs—or giving up the revenue that might otherwise flow into government coffers. But if the public is protected from being gouged on the back end—if the private sector partner is prohibited from reducing previously established service, skimping on maintenance, or charging unexpected fees—P3s can help move projects forward more expeditiously. Governments need not try to do what only private businesses have an incentive to do efficiently (if only by dint of the profit motive). And private companies need not do on their own what only government has the resources to do (with control of the public purse).

Unfortunately for American taxpayers, federal, state, and local governments have yet to figure out how to deploy P3s effectively at scale. In some states, the entire practice remains outlawed—stakeholders that do well by the more traditional "bid and build" process have stymied legislative efforts to allow state bureaucracies and local governments to be more creative. In other cases, public officials themselves aren't sold on the idea—they're fearful that sophisticated private sector bidders are going to gouge taxpayers down the line.

If P3s are simply a tool available to push complex and trying infrastructure projects past the finish line, Opportunity Democrats need to become their foremost champions. Ultimately, getting these projects done creates jobs and other economic opportunities. If we can convince voters that we know how to get projects done, infrastructure will cease to be a weight around our necks. By becoming the champions of public-private partnerships, we can turn infrastructure from crisis into opportunity.

BRIDGES TO THE FUTURE—LITERALLY

In 2013, Pennsylvania had a problem. A survey of the state's bridges came back with remarkably distressing news. Nationwide, only 7.3 percent of highway bridges were classified as being in "poor" condition, meaning that some structural element needed to be replaced. But among Pennsylvania's stock of bridges, a full 18 percent had been given that designation, constituting 4,200 different structures.[24] Engineers from PennDOT, the state's department of transportation, had been hard at work trying to bring that number down from six thousand. But as time dragged on, they hadn't been able to make a dent in the enormity of the challenge. Officials in Harrisburg, the state capital, began looking for a way to speed things along.

There were limits to what the state government could do to change the process. Few doubted that the state's larger structures were too complex to be done by a private-sector partner. But many of the smaller bridges, structures almost identical from one to the next, were a different story.

Fortunately, Pennsylvania's legislature had opened the door for public-private partnerships years earlier. And so, in September 2013, PennDOT did what no state transportation department had ever done before: officials bundled 558 small bridges together and bid out a contract to repair and rebuild *all* of them over the course of three years, and then maintain them for the following quarter century.[25] The way they structured the proposal, the private company would have a financial incentive to do a good job—if they didn't, they would be on the hook during those years to make successive rounds of repairs. Maybe more important for the state, offloading the work to private-sector companies would free PennDOT's overtaxed engineers to focus on the bigger, more complex projects.

Four companies bid on the program, which was titled the "Pennsylvania Rapid Bridge Replacement Program."[26] And for $900 million, PennDOT was able to pass responsibility for that portfolio of smaller bridges to a private partner, even as the state maintained ownership and promised to audit all the inspections.[27]

Note how this worked. Pennsylvania's P3 approach wasn't applied to *all* of the state's infrastructure projects. Some needed to be handled in house, or through the traditional cadence of bidding one contract out after the next. But when the circumstances are right and a private partner *can* reduce the cost, speed the completion, and free up resources to get other projects done more expeditiously, government *should* have the option to go that route. And that's what Democrats ought to be explaining to voters. Opportunity Democrats need to make it easier for government to serve their constituents in ways that will grow the economy. And that's exactly what public-private partnerships do when utilized correctly—they unclog the system.

THE FINAL HURDLES

America's dilapidated infrastructure is beginning to collapse under the weight of chronic underinvestment. The decay is a danger to our continued economic prosperity, national security, and growth. We have at our disposal a proven model utilized in a wide range of economically advanced countries to finance and deliver infrastructure quickly and efficiently. Yet, with some exceptions and a bit of growth, the P3 model is still stymied throughout much of the United States.

This is a case where Opportunity Democrats need to ensure that a present-day crisis does not go to waste.

The comparisons are stark. As one potential P3 investor explained not long ago,

> Canada is about one-tenth the size of the U.S. in population and GDP. This year Canada will invest about $4 billion in private money into public projects. Next year they're scheduled to do $8 billion with just 10 projects. That's $8 billion in Canada and only $7 billion in the U.S. next year. The U.S. could—and should—reach investment levels of about $80 billion if we were building at the same rate of market share as Canada. They've got it right—they're the best in the world at it—they go out to the private sector and hire lawyers and technical advisers and financial advisers...They've got competency to sit across the table from the private sector and do it with the credibility and expertise necessary to ensure the public interests are being preserved.[28]

What's gone wrong? The problem is *not* a lack of resources.

P3s are by no means free, but in many cases, the overall return on the investment (e.g., the enhanced property values, which drive additional revenue from property taxes around, say, a new train station) more than compensate for the cost. More than that, private investors today are *desperate* to put money toward infrastructure projects that will repay them with modest sums of interest over the long haul. But America can't get there from here. And as a movement demanding political reform, we need to understand why.

The first thing to appreciate is that, while P3s are often treated like newfound innovations, they were once the standard American method of building major infrastructure. It's really only since the New Deal (when Franklin Roosevelt's administration threw enormous allotments of federal funding at infrastructure through agencies like the Works Progress Administration and the Public Works Administration) that what *appears* today to be the norm (the "bid and build" system whereby a municipal or state government designs a project and then pays a contractor to construct it) came into vogue. Before that, and really through the bulk of American history, major infrastructure projects were quite frequently pursued as cooperative efforts between the public and private sectors. The Transcontinental Railroad and the Golden Gate Bridge, both built *before* the New Deal, were the result of what would today be considered P3s.[29]

But we Democrats need to be honest here. Over the last several decades, many of us have grown to assume that bid and build is the *only* proper way to fund, build, finance, and maintain major public works. And as a result, in too many cases, we've come to embrace a series of familiar norms as some sort of inviolable standard operating procedure. How to write the contracts. How to conduct the environmental and engineering reviews. How to compensate the construction companies. How to protect and compensate the workers. Even how to eliminate potential conflicts of interest.

Democrats today often dismiss P3s en masse by citing examples where they haven't worked, almost as though the bid and build model was a sure bet. But even those who believe there's a real advantage to partnering with the private sector can acknowledge that partnerships sometimes don't work out. P3s can free infrastructure projects from the bureaucratic ineptitude that can drive massive delays in projects run entirely by the public sector; they can also sometimes become entangled in complications.[30] Inevitably, similar sorts of conflicts emerge when a government bureaucracy is handling a project entirely on its own—a supplier wants to renegotiate the cost of concrete, or the newly elected mayor wants to shift the route of a road. But while those disputes can sometimes be handled in house, P3s require a different and sometimes more transparent dynamic—word is more likely to leak to the press. And that scares some public agencies away.[31]

Here's yet another challenge: Proposed P3s are often upended by an arcane problem in the American tax system. Ordinary infrastructure projects—those initiated by a government agency and completed as a traditional project—can be "bonded out." That is, the agency can issue a "municipal bond," where a private investor lends the city money to complete the project and the city pays the bondholder back (along with a tiny bit of interest) over time. Under current law, those bonds are tax-free, meaning that the money the lender gets back from the city is much more valuable than the return they would get on an ordinary loan paid back at the same interest rate. Because P3s aren't always financed with tax-free municipal bonds, they can't always take full advantage of that benefit. That means that the return investors have to recoup to do as well as they would if they simply lent the city money needs to be significantly higher, raising the costs of the project.[32]

Finally, there are the political hurdles. If a P3 *doesn't* succeed— if the project isn't completed, or it fails to accomplish its goal— the politicians who entered into the agreement are liable to be blamed for fleecing taxpayers, even if the initial intentions were entirely pure. And if the project *does* work out—if it turns out to be more profitable than originally intended, and user fees or tolls (allowed in some states, prohibited in others) are pouring in—critics are liable to complain that too much of that largesse is going toward the private-sector partner. Public officials can lose in the court of public opinion either way. So, many calculate that it's better to avoid the hassle.

But that's the whole point. In many cases, projects will never get off the ground absent a private-sector partnership. Voters are frustrated today because nothing's getting done. The federal government isn't providing the sort of money it used to send to states and local governments, much as Washington is always promising to re-up the amounts that previous administrations distributed from gas tax revenues. Year over year, federal grants to state and local governments have dropped as a share of GDP.[33] States like Missouri then refuse to raise their own revenue to invest in shoddy infrastructure, which leaves the private sector as the only viable option for demonstrating to the public that government can get things done.

That's where Opportunity Democrats can begin stepping in and pushing the process forward. We can develop models that protect taxpayers in the context of partnerships with the private sector. Already, experts have compiled lists of best practices, identified potential pitfalls, and crafted models that states and local legislators can take up, modify on the margins, and then deploy to open what we hope is a floodgate of new partnerships.[34] And as American states and localities get better at this—as they see what works and what does not—the pace of new projects can accelerate. P3s will become less the outlier and more the norm. Faith in government will begin to rise again. And our party will be able to take a share of the credit.

Supporting P3s will mean different things in different places. In some places, it will mean changing the laws. By federal standards, fewer than half of states have "broad enabling legislation." And that's a huge problem—without that sort of law on the books, states are prevented from considering P3s in situations where they haven't been explicitly authorized. Today, places as different as cobalt blue New York and ruby-red Wyoming do not have broad authority to engage the private sector, even when doing so would speed things along.[35] That needs to change.

But our reform efforts can't end there. Opportunity Democrats need to encourage those who *can* tap into the efficiencies and benefits of using P3s to take advantage when the moment is right. Pennsylvania may have more bridges teetering toward the end of their life-cycle than other states, but the Keystone State certainly isn't the only part of the country that could bundle bridge repairs together and improve their structures more expeditiously. Opportunity Democrats need to bang that drum, encouraging unresponsive bureaucracies to get more done, more efficiently.

The federal government and state legislators can both do more to help move officials in that direction. Bureaucrats who have been handling infrastructure projects the traditional way for decades can't be expected to switch to an entirely new approach overnight. For all the potential of P3s, those shaping the specifics of any proposal need to understand the implications of working in concert with a private-sector partner. They need to incorporate best practices and apply the lessons from previous P3s that have either worked out unexpectedly well or fallen short of expectations. What is too much to ask of the private sector? What represents too much of a giveaway from taxpayers?

Officials working for Canada's Province of British Columbia helped address this challenge by establishing an office that local officials could call for guidance throughout the process of crafting each individual arrangement. "Partnership BC" acts as a kind of consultant to government bureaucracies—one that gives local leaders the confidence to tackle projects in partnership with private-sector businesses. But the experts at Partnership BC don't simply hold a local government's hand through the process of shaping any prospective arrangement. Even before a locality decides to pursue a partnership, the organization serves to advertise the *possibility* of P3s in places where officials might never have considered them as an option.

That wisdom is now beginning to filter into the United States. To date, California, Michigan, and Virginia have established similar offices, and California is actually working with British Columbia, Oregon, and Washington to establish a West Coast Infrastructure Exchange.[36] The Texas Facilities Commission performs some of the same services.[37] But while that represents a promising start, it's really just the beginning. More needs to be done nationally and in various states to push P3s forward faster. If the private sector is better equipped to complete a job traditionally handled by government, we should make sure businesses are given the opportunity to get the job done. With America falling further and further behind on infrastructure, there's no time for academic debates. Opportunity Democrats need to advocate for whatever works best.

CHAPTER 4
A PORTABLE SOCIAL CONTRACT

Throughout the course of his young life, Rollin Green expected his career to follow a very specific trajectory. As a boy, he'd presumed he'd take a job with General Motors and then remain an autoworker until he retired.

The precedent had been set. His father, his grandfather, and his great-grandfather had all worked at GM's monster-sized manufacturing plant in Lansing, Michigan. So had his grandmother, a couple of uncles, and a whole variety of other friends and relatives. Building cars and trucks was, in fact, the family business. Summed together, the Greens had invested roughly three hundred years of toil in GM, building a range of Oldsmobiles, Buicks, and Cadillacs. And those years had earned generations of households the hallmarks of a middle-class lifestyle—comfortable wages, sick leave, health insurance, and generous pensions, to name a few of the perks. Rollin's father Richard explained how he viewed life as a GM employee: "If you went to work here, you were a good employee and you did things right, you'd have a job for life. My kids never had to worry about their next meal. I never thought about leaving."

But that was before the Great Recession. Not long after Rollin began working in his own right, GM's fortunes turned south.[1] In the wake of the auto giant's liquidation scare, GM was forced to change its approach to its domestic workforce. Not yet out of his early twenties, Rollin became the first member of his family to receive a GM pink slip. "It's tough," he explained to a reporter at the time. "It's always been the family business. A great-paying job, with great benefits, close to home. It was pretty much everything I ever wanted…It's provided me with whatever I had growing up."[2]

Millions of American families have faced the same dispiriting reality over the last several decades. And the shift has affected those working well beyond the automobile industry. The long-established social compact that presumed that a single job would serve as a family's permanent economic foundation has become increasingly obsolete. That's left younger workers to seek out shorter-term positions that are more tenuous and, in many cases, much less lucrative. America, in essence, is moving from a "job economy" to a "gig economy." And the gig economy has opened a loophole leaving many families without the benefits that were, a few short decades ago, standard middle-class fare.

For Democrats, this shift presents an authentic crisis, a substantive challenge, and a political opportunity. Younger workers, bereft of the sense of security that once came with full-time positions, frequently feel hopeless. They can't figure out how to replicate (much less improve on) the lifestyles their parents and grandparents enjoyed. And because neither political party has explained yet how they'd restore or maintain those benefits, Opportunity Democrats have a chance to be the first voice to address "the gig economy loophole," crafting an agenda that provides a measure of security to men and women like Rollin Green.

This isn't an issue where we need to divine a "big government" solution. And it's not as though the old job economy didn't have its liabilities. If you worked in a GM plant two generations ago, your shift might well have been determined by your seniority, rather than your convenience. Your compensation might have been determined by your years on the job, rather than the quality of your product. You might well have felt as though you were a mere cog in the wheel of an industrial machine.

Not anymore. The new gig-oriented alternative has solved for many of those frustrations. An Uber driver can work whenever she likes—and for as long as she likes. If she's particularly savvy navigating through traffic, a rider can give her a tip, explicitly tying her compensation to the quality of her performance. And if she's dissatisfied with Uber, she can seamlessly switch to another driving gig or to something else altogether—doing the odd job on TaskRabbit, for example—without losing any accrued seniority.

But that gig-centered freedom has opened an unforeseen loophole: in exchange for enduring the old shackles, workers used to be given benefits like health insurance, paid vacation time, and paid sick leave. In the new economy, much of that is being stripped away. Decades ago, for example, truck drivers were generally hired by trucking companies as full-time employees. Today, by contrast, many truckers have become contractors, picking up gigs when (and if) companies have loads they need to haul. The shift has allowed many truckers a degree of freedom, but it's also left many vulnerable to the gig economy loophole. And many resent the tradeoff.

Rene Flores, a trucker from Los Angeles, was once a full-time employee of a trucking company. But as the economy changed, he was forced to shift gears. He became a free agent, a gig worker, rather than employee. And while that had its advantages, it had its drawbacks as well. "[The trucking company executives] would send me where they wanted me to go," he explained. "They always set the price. I never did." He had to cover the cost of gas, and to keep his truck in good working order, and to purchase his own health insurance—which he chose to forgo. When he complained, the company that had been assigning him loads simply cut ties, giving his work to other contractors. "I don't have the resources to keep going for two more weeks and pay my rent and my bills," he explained.[3] And that's the essence of the loophole: the newfound freedom workers now enjoy too frequently comes at too steep a price.

Some dream of returning America to an economic system where more people have full-time jobs replete with traditional benefits. But it will be next to impossible to turn back the hands of time. First, for all the appeal of building a bridge to the past, workers would have to give up the gig economy's remarkable flexibility. Perhaps more important, employers will likely resist going back—in many cases, they've also grown accustomed to the flexibility.

That doesn't mean that, as a matter of policy, Democrats should give up the fight for fair wages, or that we should abandon the interests of men and women like Rollin Green. But the reality is that, in many cases, those sorts of benefits aren't offered anymore—even for those holding down more traditional sorts of jobs. And much as Democrats can shake their fists in the air, if voters don't believe we can provide them with those sorts of jobs, we're apt to lose our credibility if we don't adjust our thinking.

We need a new twenty-first century approach. It's time that we created a balanced system that closes the gig economy loophole with a series of *portable* benefits that are geared to the realities of today's economy. We need to provide a salve for the sense of anxiety that's now become part and parcel of American middle-class economic life. And we need to explain how portable benefits won't only benefit workers—they can unleash the next wave of American innovation.

A SHIFT IN AMERICA'S ECONOMIC FOUNDATION

From analog to digital. From industry to information. From products to services. Comprehensive discussions of America's changing economic foundation generally focus on the new and different ways companies make money in the twenty-first century. Too frequently, they ignore the dispiriting impact the changes are having on workers. The norm that existed for the post–World War II generation was clear and simple: a man (and, let's be honest, it was generally a man) would take a job and rise through the ranks of one organization through the course of his career. In return for that stability, with that single salary, a family could achieve the American Dream.

Here's the reality: that narrative simply isn't available to many workers these days. It's not that we have a jobs crisis—America boasts lots of jobs. It's just that those jobs are accompanied by a different set of benefits and expectations.

The shear breadth of the change is difficult to appreciate in full. Consider the norms that confronted college graduates who emerged into the workforce between 1986 and 1990. Five years into their careers, they averaged a mere 1.6 employers—in other words, a very substantial portion were still with the employer who had hired them right out of school. The story was entirely different for those who graduated between 2006 and 2010. Five years out, they'd averaged 2.85 employers—and nearly half had three or more.[4] As Guy Berger, an economist at LinkedIn explains: "A college degree used to slot you into a 40-year career. Now it's just an entry-level point to your first job."[5] And, of course, the same is true for those without college degrees as well.

Here's the kicker: when compared with those who have more traditional jobs, anxiety levels are more than 26 percent higher among denizens of the gig economy. That's a huge difference, and it reflects an underlying truth. While Rollin Green's relatives felt a measure of protection in the event of an unexpected challenge—unions were there to protect their interests if they were laid off, if they got sick, if they got hurt on the job—members of the gig economy are without any similar security net.[6] And the erosion of traditional benefits is having an intense impact on America's sense of well-being.

For all the additional flexibility, the gig economy loophole is leaving many American workers and their families feeling hopeless and forlorn. Many are fearful that they'll be out in the cold if they're not perpetually on the hunt for the next good opportunity. In 2018, at a point when the nation's economy was humming and unemployment was near a record low, two out of three Americans were either "worried" or "very worried" about covering their bills or expenses, and nearly two in five said their anxiety was up from the previous year.[7]

When Antonio Ivy moved from Pennsylvania to Mississippi, he applied for a job at the local Nissan plant. He figured he could get a job in the old style of the nation's auto workers—even if it wasn't unionized. But he soon discovered that Nissan was out-sourcing work inside their facility to a temp agency, paying this temporary labor a fraction of what they paid full-time employ-ees doing the same work. While Nissan employees could make twenty-four dollars per hour and claim more typical benefits, temps performing the same tasks made half that—and went without the benefits.[8] That's the environment too many workers face in America today. Is it any wonder that so many working-class Americans are so angry?

And it's not just those working "gigs." One recent survey found that nearly one in four full-time American jobs does not offer traditional benefits.[9] As a result, workers are compelled to use their cash earnings to cover their family's health care premiums, to save for their own retirement, and to cover their own income if they get sick. In other words, the gig economy loophole has begun to engulf work arrangements well beyond the confines of the gig economy. The impulse employers have to hand responsibility back to their employees is enveloping large portions of the traditional "jobs economy" as well.

Where does that leave us? The flexibility of the twenty-first century economy may be here to stay, but the simple truth is that it's not working for many workers. As Yale professor Jacob Hacker explained in the *New York Times,*

> In the mid-20th century, American corporations came to be seen as mini-welfare states, providing workers not only with job security and continuous training but also with generous health benefits and a secure retirement income. That world is gone, and it's not coming back. In short, the implicit social contract that once bound

employers, families and government has unraveled, and nothing has taken its place.[10]

From a purely political standpoint, this is where Opportunity Democrats can make a lasting mark. It's time for us to outline how we intend to provide a measure of security and prosperity to every working American and their families.

ABOVE AND BEYOND SOCIAL SECURITY

Martin Majors spent most of his hardscrabble life working as a carpenter in Opelousas, a small Louisiana town situated about an hour west of Baton Rouge. His wife Vivian had cleaned houses in the same community. The couple had worked well into their sixties, but eventually, their bodies had given out. Soon thereafter, Martin was diagnosed with Parkinson's disease, forcing Vivian to move him into a nursing home. And that left Vivian living by herself, surviving on nothing but the $600 she gets through food stamps each year and a $960 check she receives each month from Social Security. She subsists on roughly $12,000 a year, a sum that leaves her well below the poverty line.[11]

Vivian Majors's story is a window into a quiet and growing crisis throughout the country. Retirement security, once a staple feature of benefits guaranteed by a lifetime of employment, has emerged as one of the most tenuous privileges of American life. And things are slated to get worse. As a Stanford Center on Longevity report recently concluded: "Most American workers aren't saving at levels that will allow them to retire fully at age 65 at their current standard of living."[12]

The plight of American retirement security can't be ascribed to any single shift. Rather, a confluence of factors make it more difficult for Americans to live out the end of their lives in comfort and security.[13] The first is born from demographics: while America has most recently seen some backsliding on average life expectancy (due in no small part to the opioid crisis), over the last century, improvements to medicine and public health have expanded the average American lifespan by a whopping thirty years.[14] On the whole, that's good news. But longer lives come with the burden of additional retirement expenses—and that's the problem.

A study recently released out of Stanford found that baby boomers, thirty-four million of whom have *already* retired, have already largely eaten through the money that they should have saved personally for retirement. Nearly one of every three "mid-boomers" (namely those born after 1953 and before 1960) has set *nothing* aside.[15] Ten thousand turn sixty-five every day.[16, 17] And the median private savings for Vanguard Group investors who are sixty-five and older was a measly $58,000, a sum that would allow someone withdrawing money over two decades to pull out only $3,000 a year, on average.[18]

Tempting as it may be for some to castigate older Americans for failing to save enough, the truth is that many are choosing not to save for reasons that are largely beyond their control. First, and maybe most important, wages have stagnated even as health care premiums have risen, meaning that families have been forced to raid what would be retirement funding to cover present-day needs. At the same time, purchasing power has barely budged for forty years. As the Pew Research Center explained, "In real terms average hourly earnings peaked more than 45 years ago: The $4.03-an-hour rate recorded in January 1973 had the same purchasing power that $23.68 would today. Meanwhile, average health insurance costs grew by more than half between 2004 and 2014."[19] Is it any wonder why the Economic Policy Institute found that "nearly half of families have no retirement account savings at all"?[20] Or that median saving for all American families is a mere $5,000?[21]

The second leg of the retirement security stool, namely employer-supported benefits, is wobbly as well. Set aside those gig economy workers who toil without even the pretense of help—with remarkable speed, even those employers who hire people for full-time jobs have yielded to market pressure not to provide pensions. It's not always that employers are abandoning their employees altogether; rather than provide for any sort of annuity, many are choosing simply to match some portion of what employees put away in tax-advantaged retirement accounts. And the shift is widespread. Nearly three in five Fortune 500 companies offered employees old-style "defined-benefit" pensions in 1998—but only 16 percent offered any such thing in 2007, a 43 percent drop. What's more, some are actually buying out the "defined-benefit" retirement plans they've offered previous cohorts.[22] A St. Louis Federal Reserve Bank study in 2018 found that little more than 25 percent of households have a traditional pension, and only one in three have even a defined-contribution account.[23]

The upshot is that the first two legs of the retirement security stool are unquestionably compromised today. And that has put a new strain on the third. Unfortunately, the news there isn't so great either. Social Security is *also* at risk of going wobbly.

Let us be clear: That's not a reason to privatize the system, as Republicans have long wanted to do. But that doesn't mean we should hold a gauzy picture of the future. Social Security's precarious long-term finances should spur Opportunity Democrats to look at retirement security more comprehensively.[24] We won't persuade the voting public that we're equipped to solve the crisis by promising to shore up a system born in the twentieth century (though that may certainly be a part of the solution). We need to rethink the system as a whole.

The history here matters. When President Franklin Roosevelt established the program at the height of the Great Depression, his administration designed it to supplement the two other legs of the stool—to provide only as much support as a population also claiming private pensions and personal savings would need. Social Security was never designed to provide enough income by itself for Americans to maintain anything near their working-age lifestyle. Despite that reality, more than six in ten of Social Security's elderly beneficiaries depend on Social Security for more than half of their cash income today—and more than three in ten rely on their Social Security check for more than 90 cents of every incoming dollar.[25]

Here's the reality: The average benefit is only $1,326 per month.[26] That's barely more than someone makes earning the federal minimum wage *after* taxes.[27] According to *USA Today,* "[E]ight states had a higher average monthly rent for a one-bedroom apartment than the typical Social Security beneficiary would receive in a month."[28] For those without personal savings, a pension, or a retirement account, that represents an authentic disaster. What we ought to be doing, far from privatizing the system, is enhancing the benefits. But Social Security's reserves are slated to empty by 2035—a mere fifteen years from now. And as a result, Washington may be more inclined to pare back benefits than beef them up, particularly if Republicans have their way.[29]

In other words, as things currently stand, the third leg of the retirement security stool is eroding like the other two. And that, if nothing else, represents the totality of the challenge. In a world where all three legs of the traditional retirement security stool edge toward failure, how should Opportunity Democrats respond? Our mandate today is to paint a new picture of how we'll provide a better alternative to the existing system, one that avoids the pitfalls of the gig economy loophole. We need to build a new system of twenty-first century benefits.

A LEAD WEIGHT ON THE AMERICAN ECONOMY

John and Pauline Himics both grew up in New Jersey, but after college, their interests took them in divergent directions. Because he was more focused on nuts and bolts, John pursued an engineering degree. He graduated from Rowan University, then took a job at DuPont, a chemical company that remains one of the largest employers in the state of Delaware. Pauline is more of a creative type. She chose to pursue a degree in graphic design at the Pratt Institute in Brooklyn, graduated, then took a series of jobs at marketing agencies in Wilmington. During their first years out of college, the couple wanted to establish a firmer financial footing for their family, so holding positions inside established companies felt right. But then things changed; after a while, they decided they were ready to take a few more risks.

The Himicses began dreaming about starting a business of their own. So, when Pauline was twenty-two and John was twenty-three, the newlyweds established a little marketing firm, First Ascent Design, which they imagined initially as little more than a fun side hustle. For fifty dollars per month, they rented space at the Coin Loft, a small coworking facility in Wilmington. In their free time, they started hitting up networking events in search of potential clients. As John puts it, "We went around looking for people who were doing awesome things, and spending so much time doing those awesome things that they were forgetting to tell people about what they were doing."

Soon enough, First Ascent began to gain traction. Month upon month, their book of business grew. A year after finding their first client, John did the math and realized that the business added $40,000 of extra income to the family budget—a sum much more sizable than anything he could hope to earn from a raise or bonus at DuPont. He and Pauline quickly realized that their side hustle had the potential to become a more serious venture.

That gave them the courage to expand. In time, they hired two associates and two interns. They built a network of six contractors. And eventually, they moved into an office situated in a converted townhouse on North King Street, Wilmington's "lawyer's row." Five years after its founding, First Ascent was nothing less than a thriving, established business. By then, the firm had served more than a hundred clients, some in and around Delaware, but others as far away as Arizona, California, and even the UK.

Nevertheless, even amid all that success, John and Pauline still didn't feel comfortable devoting themselves full time to the thriving company. Because the cost of benefits (most notably health insurance) was so prohibitively high, John and Pauline took turns holding down jobs at big companies while the other spouse stayed at First Ascent. As of late 2019, Pauline was working during the day, not at the family company, but at the University of Delaware, which offered her (family) health insurance. Think of how crazy that is: as successful as First Ascent had become, the Himicses couldn't *both* afford to work there.

To put a label on it, the Himicses are victims of what economists call "job lock." They can't invest in the careers they *want* to pursue because they're dependent on *benefits* they can only get in their incumbent positions. John estimates that, had husband and wife been able to devote themselves full time to their joint business during the early years, the company might have grown three times as fast. They might have ten full-time employees, rather than two. But they'd never been able to take the risk because they can't afford the month-over-month expense of purchasing their own health insurance.

Unfortunately, the political class—Democrats and Republicans alike—rarely speaks to the frustration of job lock. As John explains, "It's infuriating to be in a room with decision makers or people who want to fuel innovation or fuel small businesses in Delaware but have the idea that health insurance isn't holding people back."[30] Which highlights an obvious series of questions. How many other firms aren't hiring additional employees for much the same reason? How many aggregate jobs has the American economy lost because of job lock? How much more tax revenue might flow into government coffers, to be used as investments in education, infrastructure, and more?

Job lock hasn't merely prevented John and Pauline from investing fully in their business. It has also prevented potential employees from joining their team. When John and Pauline advertise for new associates, half to two-thirds of qualified candidates opt not to pursue the opportunity when they realize that the job would come with a decent salary, ample vacation time, and a very flexible schedule—but no health insurance. The only candidates who *do* consider coming aboard have other, unrelated, ways of maintaining their coverage, or else they are so young that they're willing to take the risk of living without anything but catastrophic insurance.

The Himicses' story should loom large for those looking to reshape the Democratic Party's agenda, because we too often ignore their plight when thinking about the nation's social safety net. For the past several decades, Democrats have focused on demanding that modern-day employers pick up where the old employer-centered social contract fell off. We've tried to convince the private sector to turn back the clock and begin proffering the sorts of benefits that Rollin Green's parents and grandparents took almost for granted. In some cases, that's more than a reasonable request. But in others, the old social contract simply isn't in the cards.

Rarely if ever do we talk about breaking through the shackles that prevent people like John and Pauline Himics from making the most of their opportunities. It's time we began. Benefits tied exclusively to one particular job, be they pensions or health insurance or time off or whatever else, work too frequently to undercut the future. *Non*portable benefits pull individuals away from better opportunities, steering the broader economy away from the sort of dynamic growth that would benefit the wider population. Job lock, in other words, is undermining America's famed entrepreneurial spirit.[31] Opportunity Democrats need to replace the social safety net that prevailed during the twentieth century with something better. We need to close the gig economy loophole and end job lock by establishing a new, twenty-first century "Portable Social Contract."

BEYOND THE TREATY OF DETROIT

In the wake of the Second World War, when union leaders representing automobile workers sat down at negotiating tables across from executives from the Big Three automakers, they were faced with a choice: they could wait on Washington to come up with a government safety net that provided the nation's workers with twentieth century benefits, or they could work out an arrangement to have those benefits flow through the employers themselves. Figuring it would be more expeditious simply to work things out without waiting on the government, they went with the latter option. Their choice still reverberates today.

It's no mystery why the unions were satisfied to work out an employer-sponsored arrangement. They figured at the time that most autoworkers would spend their whole careers working the assembly lines, and that whatever benefits the government put on offer would be cumbersome to manage. At the same time, the automakers were just as happy to claim more control over their labor force. If benefits held existing workers in their jobs year upon year, the companies would avoid the costs that come with turnover. So, the two sides cut a deal that became known as the "Treaty of Detroit."[32] Benefits would flow through employers. That precedent established a norm that subsequently spread throughout the rest of the American economy.

The Treaty of Detroit might have made sense at the height of the twentieth century's industrial economy—but it is now proving increasingly obsolete. As the twin challenges of job lock and the gig economy loophole make clear, the twenty-first century economy would work more efficiently and effectively if benefits were attached to the *worker* rather than the *job*. As Opportunity

Democrats, our burden is to convince voters that we're equipped to find a way to meld some of the security tied to full-time jobs onto the flexibility that is the hallmark of the gig economy. Rather than holding a torch for some portion of the *old* system, we have to demonstrate that we have a plan to turn the page to something better and, just as important, *portable*.

Unquestionably, health care coverage is a big piece of the portability puzzle, if only because no one can reasonably claim to have made it comfortably into the middle class if they are merely one illness away from going broke. Without good health insurance, that's the reality for too many families. But a decade after President Obama pushed the Affordable Care Act through Congress, the broader question of the social safety net remains open. How, in a world where people no longer stay at a single company for the whole of their careers, will citizens be given access to the benefits their parents and grandparents expected to claim through their employer? And can the mechanisms we use to provide portable retirement security, sick leave, and more point to the way Washington can both expand health care coverage to the entire population and control costs?

Fortunately, we don't have to answer those questions from scratch. Even before Uber, Lyft, TaskRabbit, and any number of other online platforms began connecting unaffiliated workers with various projects and fares, a range of organizations and local governments had already begun putting together frameworks for the new Portable Social Contract. Their aim, in most cases, isn't to replace the system born from the Treaty of Detroit—it's to supplement it. And that's what's so exciting: Opportunity Democrats don't have to convince voters that they're going to reinvent the wheel. We simply have to explain to ordinary people that we're equipped to scale systems that have already come into being.

A NEW VISION TAKES SHAPE

The narrative around portable benefits gets confused in many cases because, to be frank, even many of the most sophisticated American citizens don't have a firm grasp on how incumbent systems of job-centered benefits work. If you've only ever had a traditional full-time job, you may have never faced the prospect of searching for a personalized package. In most companies, that's the exclusive province of the human resources department. So, as Opportunity Democrats begin to think about how to build out a Portable Social Contract, we need to paint a picture of how a reformed system *could* work. And then we need to explain why crafting a new approach would be a boon both for the economy and for workers and their families.

Take, as an example, the livery cars that ferry people around New York City. Even before Uber and Lyft made on-demand car service exponentially more popular within the five boroughs, the men and women ushering people from place to place in fancier vehicles—what New Yorkers once called "black cars" (often Cadillacs and Lincolns)—were rarely full-time employees of any one dispatch company. More often, they owned and maintained their own cars and simply contracted with various dispatchers to make their services available on demand.

For many drivers, that left a void: How could they gain access to benefits beyond setting aside a portion of the fare paid by each driver? What would happen if a driver was injured in a car accident and unable to drive for a matter of months? As full-time employees with union contracts, autoworkers in Detroit were protected in those circumstances—but livery drivers were not.

To address that problem, the drivers got together and established what became known as the "Black Car Fund." Working with dispatch companies, they forged an agreement to apply a 2.5 percent surcharge to every fare. The attendant revenue was then used to create a pool of money injured workers could claim as workers compensation. When Lyft and Uber arrived on the scene, their drivers simply joined the pool. By 2019, there were more than thirty-three thousand drivers enrolled, all of whom were eligible to draw down on the system if and when an injury prevented them from going to work.[33] In other words, a benefit typically provided through an employer was, in this case, offered as a *portable* benefit.

Years earlier, unionized construction workers and performers worked out similar sorts of arrangements. Welders and actors rarely stay employed by the same company for extended periods of time—they go from job to job. So, they each established systems whereby their employers paid a certain portion of their hourly salary to various union organizations that provided a range of benefits. Today, those benefits differ slightly from those provided through the Black Car Fund, because unionized construction workers and performers benefit from federal laws that explicitly provide for collective bargaining. But that raises a broader question: why can't a similar system apply to workers in nonunionized fields? That's where Opportunity Democrats have an opportunity to make a real contribution.[34]

PORTABLE, PRORATED, AND UNIVERSAL

It goes without saying that most Americans are not livery car drivers, actors, or welders. But as additional workers enter careers with similar rhythms—as more of us spend our working lives jumping from one employer to the next—the challenge will be to take the lessons of their experiences and apply them to wider swaths of the economy. That will require us to consider a series of trade-offs. In the world of job-locked benefits, for example, employers shouldered greater responsibility for covering the costs. But if employees are going to have more control in this new portable ecosystem, we can't let employers wash their hands of the responsibility altogether—those cutting paychecks will still need to have "skin in the game." Opportunity Democrats need to set up the framework that makes that the norm.

Here's how the twenty-first century's Portable Social Contract should be structured, in principle: It should be centered on a system that establishes "Individual Security Accounts" (ISAs) as the coin of the realm. ISAs would become repositories for the contributions that employers and employees once both made to cover benefit premiums. Industrial corporations controlled how these funds were distributed in the old system; employees will now sit in the driver's seat. To ensure continuity, employers will simply pay a prorated share of the cost. The ISAs could be scaled to the interests of each worker, and even serve as a pass-through for federal and state programs. As the Center for an Urban Future has written, "This approach could help workers in the gig economy acquire and maintain benefit coverage, while ensuring that safety net programs will continue to be funded even as more workers enter the contingent labor force."[35]

ISAs may, at first, be established among those working in certain industries, or even certain locales. But eventually, any comprehensive framework for portable benefits should be established at a national level. There's no reason, for example, that someone working various gigs on both sides of the Missouri River—namely in both Kansas City, Missouri, and Kansas City, Kansas—should be forced to navigate two separate tax and regulatory regimes. But in the absence of federal leadership, Opportunity Democrats should be making the case for state and local reforms. This is an opportunity for communities around the country to act, as a Justice Louis Brandeis saying is often paraphrased, as "laboratories of democracy."[36] And as a diversity of frameworks proliferate, those that prove most effective can be used as models for the federal government.

The key here is not simply to reclassify gig economy workers as full-time employees—or to mandate that those doing various gigs for a diversity of employers be provided benefits on the same terms as a factory worker at a GM plant circa 1959. Much as the norms established by the Treaty of Detroit hued to the realities of the twentieth century economy, the new system of portable benefits needs to be tailored to the realities of the twenty-first century. That then means, whatever the details, the system should incorporate three underlying principles, even if we only get there gradually: portability, scalability, and universality.[37]

First, whatever benefits the new systems provide (e.g., retirement security, disability insurance, workers' compensation, unemployment benefits, paid vacation, sick/family leave), those benefits need to be *portable*, even as individuals are winding their way between different realms of the economy. Americans need to be able to jump from job to job, industry to industry, and gig to gig without losing their benefits. A construction worker should be able to drive an Uber. An Uber driver should be able to act in a theater production. An actor between productions should be able to wait tables. And on and on.

That core principle is a big part of what prompted Oregon State Treasurer Tobias Read to create OregonSaves, an innovative program that serves as a publicly run retirement fund where employers can send a portion of any employee's paycheck, entirely at the employee's discretion. The program is voluntary, and unlike some more traditional retirement plans, it does not include a match. But it has created a retirement program that's simple to engage and easy to maintain for gig workers and others. That represents a vast step forward.[38]

The impact in Oregon has already been impressive. While working in the kitchen of a brewery in Cascade Locks, nineteen-year-old Ulises Orozco was making the equivalent of only $20,000 a year. When the Brewery's owner announced at the beginning of 2018 that he was going to begin putting 5 percent of each employee's paycheck into an OregonSaves account, Orozco decided not to opt out, figuring that he could take the account with him when and if he moved on to his next gig.[39] Similar stories across the state have made a big difference in participation. As of February 17, 2020, OregonSaves had 63,826 funded accounts and nearly $46 million in assets.[40]

Second, in order to ensure that ISAs are scalable, employers' costs should be *prorated*. In other words, if you work five hours at $20/hour on a project for one employer, and ten hours for an $18/hour project for another, your two employers should each be asked to contribute a fair share of the benefit costs. Within limits, *wages* should remain negotiable. But the benefit costs need to be covered by a formula that's prearranged.

Recognizing the challenge of erecting this sort of comprehensive framework, Sen. Mark Warner (D-VA) has introduced the Portable Benefits for Independent Workers Pilot Program Act, legislation that provides federal seed funding for those working to shape systems that provide continuity as individuals move between gigs and jobs.[41] He explained his thinking: "As more and more Americans engage in part-time, contract or other alternative work arrangements, it's increasingly important that we provide them with an ability to access more flexible, portable benefits that they can carry with them to multiple jobs across a day, a year, and even a career."[42] Google.org is putting private funding toward much the same goal.[43]

Third, these *portable, prorated* benefits eventually need to be *universal*. Whatever system of ISAs we build at the national level needs to be accessible to everyone, regardless of what type of job they hold. When companies abandoned traditional defined-benefit pensions for the less generous defined-contribution retirement account, they were able to take advantage of a specific loophole in the tax code known as "401(k)," which makes those contributions tax deductible. But while alternative investment vehicles exist, 401(k)s aren't available to those working in the gig economy. At some point, the new system of portable benefits should apply equally to all workers in the US economy.

That was one impetus behind Washington State's decision to create a universal paid medical leave program—one that empowers workers to take *paid* time off when they welcome a new baby into their families, need to care for a sick relative, or are forced to take medical leave themselves. For those working in traditional jobs, the program absorbs 0.4 percent of a worker's income—a third of which is covered by the employer. But as Suzi Levine, the state's commissioner of employment security explained, "Self-employed individuals, including independent contractors, sole proprietors, partners and joint ventures, may opt in to the program to receive access to benefits."[44] Today in Washington, even Uber drivers who have paid in can draw down benefits when they take time off to care for their sick kids—and that's nothing short of a revelation.

At the national level, the exact contours of the portable, pro-rated, and universal system that *should* eventually emerge need not be perfectly defined yet. As states and localities experiment, policymakers will learn more about what works, what doesn't, and how best to create a system that benefits the economy as a whole. But the bottom line, at least from a political standpoint, is that the twentieth century's Treaty of Detroit system has been rendered obsolete. Opportunity Democrats must lead the way in shaping the twenty-first century alternative.

THE POLITICS OF PORTABLE BENEFITS

No one needs to be reminded of what happened during the course of the 2016 campaign. Democrats—self-styled champions of the working class—were abandoned by a huge number of voters poised to benefit from the progressive agenda. After years of public debates, the ideological distinction between the parties was all too clear. How many times had Democrats fought for increased wages? Or universal health care? Or better benefits? Or generous paid time off? How many times had Republicans fought against them, promising nothing better than "trickle-down" economics? And yet, despite that history, legions of voters who should be solid Democrats defected to vote against Hillary Clinton.

We don't need to relitigate why Donald Trump won in 2016.

Any number of shifts could have swung the outcome the other way. But the underlying political reality can't be ignored: Much as we may believe we've established a strong legacy of championing working-class interests, working-class America isn't sold on our old agenda. Many Trump voters may desire the sorts of benefits that Democrats have espoused—but they're not convinced that our approach is equipped to deliver *for them*.

That really leaves our party with two options. We could spend the next several election cycles arguing again and again that more employers should provide more generous benefits. That would mean ignoring the realities of global competition and banging a proverbial drum for the economic system that prevailed two generations ago. Alternatively, we could try something else.

Here's what we recommend: Opportunity Democrats should become the foremost champions of a *new* system—a system built on top of the protections that already exist for the workforce. We should do our best to get voters to associate our brand with a system that will make it easier both for employers and employees to thrive in an economy fueled more by gigs and less by jobs. This is especially relevant in the long recovery period following the COVID-19 pandemic, when the demand for gigs and part-time positions will invariably expand to fill unexpected needs. That doesn't mean we should abandon individuals who still benefit from the system created by the Treaty of Detroit or let their protections be winnowed away. But it does mean that we paint a picture of an alternative route to much the same outcome.

In the end, this new ecosystem should be good for both employees *and* employers, many of whom will be partially freed from the responsibility of managing benefits (if not the responsibility to fund them). It should benefit both workers like Rollin Green *and* employers like John and Pauline Himics. Most important, it should turbocharge the economy, allowing entrepreneurs to find better talent and for talented employees to find better jobs.

Whether or not Americans are thrilled with the shifts that define the twenty-first century economy, they're the ones out looking for jobs and trying to build their own prosperity. If we can be the party that points the way toward a new system that works explicitly for them, they will eventually respond. This is a chance for Opportunity Democrats to redefine our party's legacy and vision. More than that, it's an opportunity to speak to a population of voters whom we need if we're going to win elections on a consistent basis.

CHAPTER 5

EVERYDAY ENTREPRENEURS

Optimism. If any single word defines Silicon Valley, that may very well be the one. At a moment when the American Dream seems increasingly out of reach for so many, those making it rich inside America's tech bubble seem to live a very different reality. Democrats have long struggled to straddle that dichotomy. On the one hand, we view ourselves as champions of those who need a hand up, lamenting time and again the impact of income inequality. But in red America, we're associated with the wealthy set that's making it big on the coasts.

The election result in 2016 made clear enough the approach we've taken recently to this issue hasn't worked politically. We need to reassess. Much as we should celebrate the growth of the nation's technology sector, when we're building our economic agenda, we need to look beyond Sand Hill Road. We need to side squarely with the men and women running small businesses throughout the rest of the country. In other words, if we're going to be the party of economic growth, we need to become the party of *everyday entrepreneurs*.

Their struggle is real. Step into a conversation with someone developing plans to "monetize" a new app, or "build a platform" for a streaming service, and you'll most likely note that their tone is markedly different from that of a family considering whether or not to expand their small dry-cleaning business. Many of Silicon Valley's founders presume that the world is their proverbial oyster—that they do themselves a disservice if they fail to explore even the craziest ideas. But innovators everywhere else are left more often to act from a defensive crouch. Can they hack it in a global economy? Is it even worth trying? The entrepreneurial ecosystem is cold in too much of America, and that's a huge problem—one Opportunity Democrats need to address.

This is a topic on which Democrats have a disastrous track record largely because we've failed to pay attention. In recent years, even as the country has grown more skeptical of tech billionaires, reverence for the small business community has remained strong.[1] The nation's middle class intuitively understands and respects the risk-taking that comes with striking out on your own. Moreover, they know that entrepreneurialism is the best way to unlock widespread economic growth, both over the short and long term. The Davos crowd may not be popular in a lot of America, but the nation still reveres those who pull themselves up from nothing while relying on little more than worldly intuition and tireless work ethic.

However inexplicably, our party has largely set that narrative aside. Rather than talking about small business success as a hallmark of the American Dream, we often describe entrepreneurs almost as though they were charity cases seeking out the government's goodwill. That's a huge mistake, because it misses the truth of the entrepreneurial spirit. If we're going to establish the Democratic Party once again as a beacon of a middle-out economic agenda, we need to make sure that those working in small businesses see us as a party that wants government to help them thrive—not as some sort of benefactor, but as a dynamic partner. We need to build a governing agenda that treats small businesses as the economic engines that they are. And we need to pointedly explain, as we strive to make the public sector a better partner for entrepreneurs, here's what we intend to do *for you*.

Here's the central question: can someone with a marketable idea get their hands on whatever they need to make a go of their own tenacity and hard work? That's not a topic you hear Democrats talk about much on the campaign trail. Our candidates tend to focus instead on the scourge of greed. We're prone to color those who have succeeded in business not as paragons, but as leeches on the greater good. Not every entrepreneur is a hero. But when we paint with such a broad brush that we seem to be excoriating anyone who has made it big, we demonize the very figures many Americans want to become. How can we claim to be the party of entrepreneurs when we're so quick to pillory those who have managed to thrive within the system of free enterprise?

Imagine the experience someone living in, say, a Midwestern suburb has when they walk into a local bank and fill out a small business loan application. In that moment, they're rarely thinking about the compensation structure for the bank's top officers. They're unlikely to be focused on anything other than whether or not they'll be approved—and whether or not the financial terms on offer will work for their particular venture. If we can make a clear-cut case specifying what we'll do specifically for entrepreneurs, legions of persuadable voters will give Democratic candidates a second look.

To that end, we need to become champions of people like Natasha Griswold. Griswold isn't a tech entrepreneur. She's a woman of color who, while five months pregnant and newly evicted from her apartment, started a traveling salon business that serves residents of nursing homes.[2] After outfitting ten "Elder Hair Care" salon units, she built a business that now turns a profit and does a community a real service.[3] Griswold's is the classic American story. With little beyond a good idea and a willingness to put in some hard work, she built something important. Democrats need to celebrate her journey. More than that, we need to ensure that more Natasha Griswolds are able to live their dreams. We need to lay out in clear prose exactly what we plan to do *for them*.

This challenge doesn't center on fat cat financiers. It's not tied up in any CEO's golden parachute. In many ways, it's not even about Wall Street (though big banks could certainly do more to help companies located in the middle of America). The Democratic Party's small business platform needs to make clear that we know there are unrealized good ideas floating around communities *all over* America—not just on the coasts. For every budding tech entrepreneur who gets an encouraging word at a conference in San Jose, there are dozens of Americans throughout the rest of the country frustrated that no one will back a venture they've been thinking about for years. It's high time that we bridge that gap. Opportunity Democrats need to prioritize a campaign to expand access to capital.

HOW THIS IS *SUPPOSED* TO WORK

Imagine you've got a great idea for a new small business. Perhaps there's a little corner of your neighborhood that isn't served by a good tailor. Or you're convinced the millennials moving into a newly developed subdivision would patronize a new, hip coffee shop. Maybe you're already a small businessman—you and your wife own a restaurant, an accounting firm, a clothing store—and you want to open a second location. Where can you get your hands on the cash you'd need to get your new business idea off the ground or to expand a company that's already bustling?

Shark Tank viewers might presume that any entrepreneur's first stop is to seek out a "venture capitalist," namely someone willing to provide an infusion of cash in return for a stake in the business. In some corners of the American economy, that's accurate. Venture capital is prevalent in the tech community for one simple reason: tech businesses can become immensely valuable extremely quickly. Companies such as Facebook or Dropbox expanded both rapidly and astronomically, making the venture capitalists' early investments look, in financial parlance, like "a hockey stick." And that's why venture capital makes sense for businesses that are slated to take off in short order: the business may fail—but if it succeeds, that early investment is likely to pay off many times over.

Unfortunately, most coffee shops and accounting firms rarely grow like that. As the Center for an Urban Future explained in one recent report, "[Venture Capital] investors usually seek returns of 30 times their investment, which is virtually impossible for independent small businesses."[4] So *most* American entrepreneurs, and certainly most entrepreneurs looking to build companies that are unlikely to scale like a tech company, are left to look for other sources of money. As with someone looking to purchase a home or finance an education, they seek out loans. Those loans don't come from people hoping to make a bundle overnight. They come from banks and other financial institutions that take a much more conservative approach to lending.

Here are the facts: More than nine out of ten entrepreneurs thinking of starting a business (that comprises more than just a single proprietor working out of their home) end up needing some sort of financing to get off the ground. Less than 1 percent receive that funding from venture capital. So, *Shark Tank* isn't remotely reminiscent of what most small businesses experience in their search for funding. Perhaps that isn't shocking—it is, after all, a television show.

But the most frequent source of small business seed funding may be a surprise to most readers. The vast majority of entrepreneurs don't even approach a third-party to solicit funding; they end up lending their own personal money to their new venture.[5] That suggests that *having* money is a huge leg up when you're looking to *make* money.

So, what do you do if you don't have enough savings to get your business off the ground—or you don't want to raid your daughter's college fund in pursuit of a business that might not work? You're often forced to look elsewhere—namely to a lender. And that's where entrepreneurs often run into trouble. In far too many circumstances, banks and financial institutions aren't lending in the places where people have good ideas but insufficient means to grow them. If Opportunity Democrats are going to advocate in earnest for the nation's frustrated entrepreneurs, we need to address three separate challenges.

The first is that, in vast expanses of America, lenders simply aren't available. We'll see this later when discussing the plight of Danielle Baker, a rural farmer in North Carolina. The second (and possibly even more daunting) challenge centers on the fact that lenders today reject a greater percentage of small business loan applications than they have in years past, making start-up funding that much more elusive.[6] And third, even when lenders *do* accept an application, the terms are often steep.[7] Recent research reveals that a full third of small businesses considering whether to grow choose not to apply for capital, in many cases because they don't think they can afford the interest on a loan.[8] Is it any wonder why so many would-be entrepreneurs decide to sit on their dreams?

It's not like this across the whole of the economy. Larger businesses, for example, have much more ready access to capital. As the think tank Third Way has reported, "Since the [Great Recession] ended, big businesses have posted a 35% increase in loans, as small businesses have seen a 9% decrease."[9] Because finance is often a zero-sum game, big companies' success is the small business community's loss. What accounts for the change? For many big banks in particular, the costs associated with making a $1 million loan to a big business do not differ substantially from those associated with making a $100,000 loan to an entrepreneur, but the larger loan stands to bring the bank much more revenue. For that same reason, because most small businesses don't need nearly so much capital, big banks are choosing more frequently to turn their backs, deeming those smaller loans to be unworthy of their time.[10] As Third Way found, "Many of the largest financial institutions have stopped making loans to businesses with less than $2 million in revenue and stopped making loans less than $100,000. Instead, large financial institutions direct loans of less than $100,000 to their small business credit card products that earn higher yields."[11]

When the Center for an Urban Future looked into the challenges facing the small business community in New York City, they found much the same problem. As one report explained,

> Once small businesses tap start-up grants, friends and family loans, and community bank loans, they struggle to secure financing for amounts ranging from $50,000 to $500,000. Microfinance organizations top out at around $15,000, and most community banks do not make loans greater than $50,000 or $100,000, regardless of the company's revenue stream. At the same time, big banks do not make small business loans for less than $500,000.[12]

But getting a loan offer is just the first hurdle. Once a bank accepts your application, they provide terms, and entrepreneurs frequently suffer because the interest rates associated with the loans for which they *do* qualify are much steeper than they would be if their businesses were more established. By one estimate, in late 2019, traditional bank loans ranged from 3 percent to 6 percent APR. But SBA loans, subsidized by the federal government, ranged from 7.5 percent to 10 percent. Some business lines of credit ranged up to 36 percent. Invoice financing can range up to 60 percent. And merchant cash advances can rise to a remarkable 150 percent.[13] As a result, even when capital is accessible to small businesses in theory, it really isn't in practice.

While limiting access and charging remarkably high interest rates may represent a savvy shift for bankers, the change has undoubtedly been a drain on the American economy writ large. How do we know? Small businesses around the country are failing.

As Third Way has put it, "Partly as a result of less credit, more than 2,100 counties in America suffered a net loss of businesses between 2005 and 2015, shedding a net total of 200,000 private-sector businesses and 1.2 million private-sector jobs over that decade." Start-ups, a category of business that represented 13 percent of firms in the United States as recently at 1980, represented a mere 8 percent in 2014.[14] Remember, seven in ten new jobs in America are born from small business, so the ripple effects are profound.

What is the crucial takeaway from all this data? Most important, we should realize that the crisis enveloping the nation's small businesses is not being driven by a dearth of ideas, or a failure of tenacity, or a dwindling capacity to compete with businesses overseas. It's literally that, in many cases, entrepreneurs can't find the money to get their businesses off the ground or to scale successful ventures. This is Economics 101: the lending supply isn't meeting small business demand. For entrepreneurs, *that's* the challenge that Opportunity Democrats need to solve.

UNDERMINING THE AMERICAN ECONOMY

It's impossible to know *exactly* how many jobs have been snuffed out by insufficient access to capital through the years, or how many points the crisis has taken off the nation's GDP. But we have a wealth of examples of what *can* happen when the spigots open and worthy applicants have opportunities to build their dreams. Here's a question we really ought to be asking as we drive our agenda: how many untapped Natalie Youngs exist in America today? Hers is a story worth remembering.

In her late thirties, Young fell into addiction. By the time she was fired from a high-end restaurant in Telluride, Colorado, she'd been living in the grip of cocaine for well over a decade. As she explained two decades later, "I woke up the next day, when I actually lost the job, and I thought, 'I'm going to die if I don't get out.'" Facing those dire circumstances, she managed to scrape together enough money to cover a stint in rehab, and then found a place to stay at a sober house in Las Vegas. What happened next was a testament to what *can* happen if resilient people are given a chance to succeed.

Over the course of several years, while maintaining her sobriety, she worked her way up from broiler cook to sous-chef at the Eiffel Tower Restaurant at Paris Las Vegas. She subsequently bounced around between several other Las Vegas restaurants, holding down jobs with varying degrees of success. The experiences taught her how to run a business and how to serve meals that would draw a deep well of happy customers. Eventually, she decided she wanted to strike out on her own; that's when she caught an unexpected break. Zappos CEO Tony Hsieh had decided to invest $350 million in what was called the "Downtown Project," a campaign to improve the business environment in Las Vegas. As part of Hsieh's initiative, Young received an interest-free $225,000 loan to establish her own restaurant, Eat.[15] That was all she needed to get started.

In the months immediately following Eat's opening, Young struggled to keep her own finances in order. Cash flow was tight before the restaurant established its now sterling reputation. But a year later, Eat had brought in enough business to enable Young to repay the loan. That's when she began to think about branching out. Young opened a second restaurant, Eat Summerlin. Then she established a catering business, Chow.[16] She is now, by almost every measure, a wildly successful entrepreneur. She's smart, talented, and tenacious. But none of it would have been possible without *access to capital*.

Not every entrepreneur will be so successful—indeed, Young might have failed if she'd made any number of missteps along the way. But by the same token, not every loan necessarily needs to lead to a blockbuster business to be considered a success. Take another example: Diane Cutler and Andy Zivinsky, both long-time bicycle enthusiasts, noted during a visit to Bryson City, North Carolina, that the small town didn't have a bike shop to serve the tourists exploring the world-class trails nearby. Could they successfully tap that underserved market? Convinced they had a viable business plan, the question became whether they could afford to leave their jobs and devote themselves exclusively to the bike shop. After doing some analysis, they decided to take the plunge.

It took a lot of work. But after getting a $70,000 loan from a credit union, they set up Bryson City Bicycles. A decade later, the business was pulling in $250,000 in annual revenue. As Cutler explained in 2018: "We are making a living—not a killing—and we work more hours than ever before. But we do the things we love more often. We bike, hike, fly-fish and bird-watch, and we're happier than we've ever been."[17] *That* is, by many measures, the American Dream—and it's the sort of story Democrats should seek to make possible for more entrepreneurs around the country. Cutler and Zivinsky's success is largely due to their own business acumen and hard work. But, again, it wouldn't have happened without the necessary financing.

It's not just new businesses that struggle to secure capital. Having established a successful cheesesteak restaurant in Kansas City and opened a successful second location, Shelton Ross wanted to open a third. But despite his track record of success, he *still* couldn't get the bank loan he needed to expand. "I showed them what we were expecting to make, showed them our potential, and we're still being turned down," he explained at one point. Eventually, Ross secured a loan through AltCap, a nontraditional lender focused on underprivileged neighborhoods, and his third location thrived. But it's no mystery why he came away from those rejections seething. Many entrepreneurs feel almost as though the world of finance is more of a barrier to their success than a partner. And that's true across the country.

Two years after Lula Luu established Paducah, Kentucky's Fin Gourmet, a business selling fish and seafood to high-end restaurants, she decided she wanted to expand. To grow, she would need a loan. But as she searched for capital, she was turned down time and again. Luu had founded the business not only because she knew restaurants needed quality seafood, but because she wanted to provide jobs for communities in need, namely Louisiana shrimpers during their off season, residents of domestic violence shelters, and people recently released from prison. Because she was pursuing a "second bottom line"—that is, her intention was to make both a profit *and* a difference—lenders were hesitant to offer her the funds she needed to grow. As the Kauffman Foundation, a leading nonprofit championing entrepreneurship, explained, "Lenders from large banks in Louisville and Nashville said that, as a two-year-old business, Fin was too risky; venture capitalists said the company was not high-growth enough for equity funding."

Eventually, Luu managed to secure some funding by partnering with a social impact-oriented financing firm, Village Capital, which had built a financing mechanism that aimed to earn investors three times return on whatever they put into the business, a return much more modest than what they might expect through a more traditional investment.[18, 19, 20] But the amount of time and energy Luu had to invest in the search for capital is an important part of the problem. What if she hadn't applied to Village Capital? What if a similarly hard-charging entrepreneur never finds a firm willing to craft a similar solution? How many businesses in places like Paducah, Kentucky, *aren't* growing, despite their underlying potential, because their proprietors can't find investors? How many would-be entrepreneurs with good ideas simply give up?

WHERE THE SPIGOT DOESN'T FLOW

Admittedly, some political issues are vexingly complicated. It can be hard to explain in a stump speech how interest rates work, or why trade deficits fail to be a good way to measure the economy's vitality. But when it comes to small business lending, you don't need to be a member of MENSA to understand that a business can't grow without some up-front investment. You can't make something from nothing. Importantly, if you don't *think* you'll be able to get your hands on start-up capital, you may not give it a go in the first place—even if your idea is a guaranteed winner.

Silicon Valley's venture capitalists are sometimes so confident that a certain tech-savvy programmer will come up with a big idea—or at least that the upside potential of any given loan is worth the downside risk—that they don't even wait for an idea to germinate. They basically throw money at young talent. But that story is the exception, not the rule. Throughout the rest of the country, many struggle to find start-up money of any sort—a loan, a partner, whatever the arrangement might be—even when they're sitting on what is unquestionably a great idea.

Head in from the coasts and you're likely to discover that even the most established entrepreneurs often struggle to access capital when they're considering whether to scale or expand. Big banks reject nearly three in four small business loan applications (a marginal improvement on the 87 percent rejection rate that prevailed as recently as 2014[21]), and small banks reject nearly one in two.[22] That points to a dispiriting economic diagnosis: even in moments when the economy is purportedly booming, in most of America, good ideas are being starved for funding.

It would be one thing if these small businesses were a marginal factor in the American economy—if big businesses were the main attraction, and small businesses were more of a sideshow. But, in fact, small businesses are the overwhelming source of the nation's most prolific dynamism. The US economy boasts nearly thirty million small businesses—and those small businesses employ roughly one of every two workers. Small businesses are responsible for *70 percent* of job growth. So ensuring that these companies have opportunities to expand is critical not just to the proprietors, but to the economy as a whole.[23]

These facts may be glossed over in Washington, where the Small Business Committee is considered a B-level assignment at best. But entrepreneurs are well aware of what they're up against. When a 2018 Pepperdine University survey of business executives asked whether they "thought it would be easy or difficult to raise new financing in the next six months," nearly *half* of small businesses (those with less than $5 million in annual revenue) reported that it would be difficult. At the same time, merely a third of big business executives (those with between $5 million and $100 million in annual revenue) gave the same answer.[24]

None of this is to argue that lenders should be required to

approve every loan application. Bank officers inevitably reject some doozies. Nor is it any mystery why big businesses have a better approval rate—they carry less risk. Banks make smaller profits on smaller loans, and small businesses have less collateral to offer as a guarantee.[25] But if there's *always* been some sort of delta between the access big and small business had to capital, the Great Recession widened the chasm into one that, for many would-be entrepreneurs, has made starting (or expanding) a small business next to impossible. While small business lending grew at a steady rate between 2001 and 2007, it fell off by 60 percent in the wake of the 2008 financial meltdown.[26] And that shift continues to reverberate. In all likelihood, the same problem will reoccur following the COVID-19-related financial crisis.

In 2017, the *Wall Street Journal* dispatched two reporters to a small town in North Carolina to see how banking had evolved in rural America through the years. What they uncovered was what might be known as a credit desert. If you travel to midtown Manhattan, you'll be able to spot a bank branch from nearly any street corner. Roxobel, North Carolina, by contrast, doesn't boast a single financial storefront. As a result, when Danielle Baker, a local family farmer, went looking for a loan from Southern Bank, which had long served her and her family business, she had to drive a few towns over. When she applied to a larger bank, PNC, she had to travel even further. Both banks turned Baker down, claiming that, despite years in operation, her business was too specialized. Asked about access to credit, Baker simply responded: "If you are not a big company with tons of assets and a big bank account, they just overlook you."

Baker eventually secured the financing she needed for her family business—but not from a bank. She was left to solicit a nonprofit lender located in Raleigh, the state capital situated more than one hundred miles away. Because her lender was a nonprofit rather than an ordinary bank, Baker couldn't drive up to a branch like most business owners working out of a thriving city. Instead, she had to drive to a town nearly twenty miles away to deposit the earnings she took in each day, or to grab cash to stock her register. Worse, to do anything more substantial, she had to drive all the way to Raleigh.[27]

Baker's plight might not seem like a major threat to the American economy. Perhaps Roxobel's sputtering economy simply doesn't justify a bank branch anymore. But what too many of us fail to appreciate is that Baker's plight isn't a one-off—it's a massive trend. As a report from the Woodstock Institute noted in early 2017,

> The number of…loans [provided] nationally to small firms (businesses with gross revenues under $1 million) was just under 5 percent lower in 2014 than in 2001, and 51 percent lower than the peak in 2007, while the total dollar amount of those loans in 2014 was down nearly 47 percent from the amount in 2007 and down over 28 percent since 2001.[28]

That's a problem for small businesses in nearly every corner of America, whether it's rural North Carolina or suburban Wisconsin. The American economy simply can't grow if capital is limited to thriving communities on the coasts. Entrepreneurs of every stripe need a fair shot at achieving their dreams. And Opportunity Democrats need to help make those dreams into realities.

WHERE IT HURTS THE MOST

As you might expect, the struggle to find capital isn't the same for every American community. Some suffer more than others. From a political perspective, that's particularly important because it connects a very powerful economic challenge to a political strategy equipped to propel Democrats to nationwide victory. As we'll see, the greatest frustration centers among demographics that are crucial to the Democratic Party's ability to build a broad-based coalition in the decades to come. An agenda that expands access to capital will draw voters from blue, red, and purple America together behind Democratic candidates.

Let's begin with young people. Because most have yet to climb into the upper ranks of any established business (and, if they're stuck out on their own, their self-propelled venture is unlikely to have grown to mammoth proportions), millennial entrepreneurs are more likely to need capital if they're going to found or scale a business of their own making. For that reason, winnowing opportunities to access capital have left them disproportionately cut off from opportunity.

The good news is that many millennials boast that they are less tied than previous generations to established banks, meaning that they're more willing to seek out other sources of credit—loans and equity connected to credit unions, private equity, and venture capital firms. But even then, one recent report found them increasingly frustrated:

> Millennials report having been denied capital in the past year at a higher rate than their older peers—59% of Millennials were denied capital in the past 12

months compared to 43% of Gen Xers and 27% of
Baby Boomers. 49% of Millennials say they are concerned or very concerned about accessing capital for
current business needs compared to 39% of Gen Xers
and 27% of Baby Boomers.[29]

Many surely would be interested to know what Democrats will
do *for them*. We need to supply an answer.

Female entrepreneurs are also facing increasingly long odds
in the search for funding. When Dana Donofree, a breast cancer
survivor, established a successful lingerie line in Philadelphia for
female survivors and women battling cancer, she quickly found a
market hungry for her products. But when she began exploring ways
to launch a third line, she struggled to land the $35,000 loan that
her business needed before accepting an invitation to New York
Fashion Week. The bank with whom she had a long-standing rela-
tionship turned down her application. That forced her to network in
search of other potential lenders. It was only through tenacity and
perseverance that she eventually found a lender willing to support
her business's growth.[30] Had she given up the search, she might
have lost out on the opportunity to grow her brand.

A report by Experian found that Donofree's experience isn't
unique. A disproportionate share of female small business owners
face steep hurdles when seeking access to capital. Potential lenders
often rate female candidates as "less credible" or "less legitimate"
than similarly credentialed men, even after they've launched their
companies and proven they can turn profits. Studies have shown
that female founders are more frequently forced to use personal
savings to capitalize their businesses. And maybe most remarkably,
the extra hurdles aren't exclusive to the moments when men are

making lending decisions—female lenders *also* prefer to make loans to male applicants.[31] Many female entrepreneurs would surely be interested to know what Democrats will do *for them.*

As the *Wall Street Journal* has reported, entrepreneurs of color face similarly long odds—though in their collective case, the barriers may be even steeper. In 2014, Maurice Brewster, an African American small businessman with a years-long track record running a limousine and transportation company out of Redwood City, California, applied to Wells Fargo for a $250,000 loan. He was rejected; the bank justified their decision by citing Brewster's insufficient collateral. The rejection might have made sense if Brewster was just starting out. But the businesses had been in operation for a dozen years. Moreover, the company had thrived in good times, with its struggles emerging amid the worst financial catastrophe since the Great Depression. Nevertheless, Brewster couldn't get a loan.

Brewster's experience reflects a broader postrecession trend: when big banks pared back their lending to small businesses, the shift disproportionately impacted minority-owned enterprises. Four years after the financial crisis, the *Wall Street Journal* analyzed the universe of loans backed by the federal government's Small Business Administration during the recovery. A mere 1.7 percent—$328.5 million of a total $23.09 billion—had gone to black borrowers, despite the fact that a full 7 percent of American business owners are black. *Before* the crash, minority-owned businesses had done much better, securing 8.2 percent of the money loaned out in 2008. African American–owned businesses fell off even more steeply than those owned by Latinx and Asian Americans.[32] That's a remarkable, and revealing, shift. It's likely many minority business owners want to know what Democrats will do *for them.*

Millennials, women, and minorities: historically, those demographics tend to favor Democrats. But capital access isn't an issue that exclusively befuddles Democratic corners of the electorate. It also affects some of the reddest parts of the country. As typified by Danielle Baker's plight in Roxobel, North Carolina, those living in rural and exurban American communities, though generally more conservative, face many of the same hurdles that tend to trip up entrepreneurs elsewhere. Moreover, residents of rural America actually found businesses more readily than their entrepreneurial counterparts in other parts of the country. And here's the thing: a recent survey found that nearly one in five identified limited access to capital as one of the three biggest external barriers to their success.[33] That just goes to show that on this issue, red, purple, and blue voters sing from the same hymnal. But to date, Democrats haven't answered back.

Rural voters have good reason to complain. As the *Wall Street Journal* reported,

> The value of small loans to businesses in rural U.S. communities peaked in 2004 and is less than half what it was then in the same communities, when adjusted for inflation…In big cities, small loans to businesses fell only a quarter during the same period, mainly due to large declines in lending activity during the financial crisis. *Adjusted for inflation, rural lending is below 1996 levels.*[34] [Emphasis added]

What's going on here? Shifts in the financial industry have been devastating to the community banks that once served rural parts of America, many of which have folded or been sold to larger banks. Why does that matter? Smaller, regional banks are often more willing to lend to rural small businesses because they know the business owners personally, unlike big banks, which are farther removed.[35] And since the Great Recession, community banks are down more than 40 percent.[36] That phenomenon is true in blue America as well. As the Center for an Urban Future found in New York alone:

> Small banks, with assets of less than $10 billion, have been disappearing in New York and across the United States. From 1992 to 2011, according to the state's Department of Financial Services, the number of New York City community banks fell from 299 to 169. [Nationally, the number has fallen from 14,000 in the 1980s, to fewer than 7,000 in 2014.[37]] The number of banks with less than $100 million in assets declined even more sharply, from 99 to 22 over the same period. The assets of community banks also fell precipitously, from $237 billion to $166 billion. Deposits, which are more important for small banks than big banks because of their more limited activities, declined from $188 billion to $130 billion.[38]

The nationwide decimation of smaller banking institutions has been ominous everywhere, but the impact has been most noticeably felt in places that are already struggling. Between 2012 and 2014, low-income census tracts across the country were home to more than 9 percent of the nation's businesses. But they received less than 5 percent of the nation's business loans.[39] This is an issue where government *can* play a constructive role. Opportunity Democrats need to convince the public that we're prepared to do something about a challenge we can no longer afford to ignore.

THE ENTREPRENEUR AGENDA

So, what exactly can Democrats do for small business owners and would-be entrepreneurs? We begin by building an agenda that gives them the resources they need to unlock a new wave of broad-based, middle-out economic growth. If the Green New Deal was intended specifically to deal with climate change, the Entrepreneur Agenda should be shaped to spread access to capital. We need to make clear that we intend to give Americans with great ideas all over the country the confidence required to make a go of their own free-standing businesses. If we're going to convince the electorate that Democrats are the party of growth, we need to explain to the small business community exactly what we'll do *for them*.

We should begin by reorienting the primary tool the federal government uses to spur banks to open their coffers to innovators, namely the Small Business Administration's (SBA) flagship "7(a)" program, established in 1953, which limits a bank's losses in the event that a small business fails to repay a loan.[40] The program has long had its heart in the right place. But as the evidence above makes clear, 7(a) is no longer getting the job done. When the program was originally conceived, the world of finance was completely different. The risks bankers associated with entrepreneurs occupied a different place in the constellation of lending opportunities—compared to today, they were more attractive. Given that change, Opportunity Democrats need to craft a plan to provide new and improved incentives, and then to explain our approach to the public at large. So let's get to work.

First, at a time when community banks are disappearing and larger banks are refusing to make the sorts of loans entrepreneurs demand, the federal government should sweeten the pot. Guarantees for loans made in amounts between $150,000 and $700,000 should rise from 75 percent to 85 percent. That is, if a qualifying bank provides a loan to a small business and the small business is unable to repay the loan, the bank should be protected from losing more than 15 percent of its investment. That way, if an established lender has a choice between providing a single $5 million *un*guaranteed loan to a large business or, alternatively, ten $500,000 loans guaranteed by the federal government to several small businesses, the latter cohort may become comparatively more attractive. At the same time, the SBA should reduce the fees it assesses for each guarantee—costs that are inevitably borne by the borrowers. Loans below $150,000 should not be assessed any fee whatsoever, and those that rise to $700,000 should be limited to 1 percent.[41]

Second, Washington should eliminate some of the restrictions that prevent many 7(a) applicants from meeting the eligibility requirements. Most notably, when 7(a) was born, a much smaller proportion of potential applicants held student debt, so limiting the pool of applicants to those who had already paid off their student loans did not affect a large proportion of the population. Since then, however, as educational costs have risen, more Americans—and particularly more *young* Americans—have had to assume debt in advance of earning their degrees.[42] The amount of outstanding student loan debt has doubled in aggregate over the last ten years.[43] It's not that the federal government should eliminate standards altogether; taxpayer dollars shouldn't be guaranteeing loans sure to fail. But clearly, given changes within the community of applicants, the requirements need reform.[44]

Third, Democrats should announce a soup-to-nuts review of the financial regulations that impact small businesses. Too often, we are seen as the party of red tape because, while we're eager to publicize plans to put new mandates on companies big and small, we're rarely seen looking back to weigh whether old regulations remain appropriate in the twenty-first century marketplace. Regulators see their role as guardians of the common good—and that's perfectly right. No one wants to recreate the regulatory lapses that opened the door to the financial collapse of 2008. But the common good is not served when arcane regulations are left on the books, forcing the sort of unnecessary and useless scrutiny that can curtail an entrepreneur's ability to grow their business. A growing economy is *also* a public good. Regulators should prioritize both protecting consumers *and* helping companies thrive.

Fourth, programs that the SBA maintains to target underserved markets should be made permanent. Authorization for the Community Advantage Pilot Program expires in 2022; the program, which expands the guarantees offered for loans extended to businesses in underserved communities, will need a new mandate from Congress if Washington intends to continue providing a hand up to veterans, entrepreneurs of color, and women in small business.[45] Similarly, Congress should provide even more support for the Minority Business Development Agency and for Small Business Development Centers and Women's Business Centers, which work to help marginalized entrepreneurs grow and advocate for their interests with policymakers and others.[46, 47, 48, 49]

Fifth, Opportunity Democrats should expand Washington's efforts to build up entrepreneurs beyond the work of the

Small Business Administration. The SBA does an admirable (if insufficient) job overcoming the hurdles that leave minority and female-owned businesses at a disadvantage in heavily populated urban areas. The agency has a much more limited presence in rural America. The Department of Agriculture (USDA), by contrast, maintains Rural Business Development Grants and a Rural Microentrepreneur Assistance Program, which together provide grants, lending, and technical assistance to entrepreneurs outside the nation's metropolitan areas.[50, 51] USDA also administers the Intermediary Relending Program, which "provides 1 percent low interest loans to local lenders of 'intermediaries' that re-lend to businesses to improve economic conditions and create jobs in rural communities."[52] As we reach out beyond the limits of traditionally blue America, Opportunity Democrats need to explain how they will strengthen and grow those programs as well.[53]

Sixth, Opportunity Democrats should find ways to help small businesses tap funding streams available through credit unions. In 1998, Washington imposed a new regulation capping lending to small businesses to 12.25 percent of a credit union's total assets. That limit now appears arbitrary, a vestige of an old regulatory regime that serves only to reduce the competition traditional banks face when entrepreneurs seek out a loan. As Rohit Arora, who cofounded Biz2Credit and writes occasionally about the state of lending recently argued, "Increased competition among lenders will free up capital. If it happens, entrepreneurs who want to borrow money to grow their businesses will ultimately benefit."[54]

Seventh, Washington should increase funding for Community Development Financial Institutions, banks that operate overwhelmingly in underserved communities. While the Clinton Administration created a federal fund at the Treasury Department to increase capital at CDFIs around the country, government backing would have a much more powerful impact if the well ran deeper. Moreover, Opportunity Democrats should champion and make permanent the New Market Tax Credit, a program that has already attracted more than $60 billion in loans to companies in areas of the United States that are struggling economically.[55]

Finally, Opportunity Democrats need to find allies in the private, philanthropic, and nonprofit sectors willing to bridge the gaps that limit the small business community's access to capital. Mindful never to create an unintentional credit bubble, the nonprofit community could build a responsible mechanism to pool small business loans together, minimizing the downside risk from any single loan. Could philanthropic organizations augment the work that the government is already doing to enhance entrepreneurialism in places that have been deprived of capital, like Opportunity Zones?[56] With capital so limited, policymakers need to embrace newfound creativity.

A RARE POLITICAL OPPORTUNITY

It didn't take much—just a pottery wheel and a $5,000 kiln. With that, Emily Reinhardt made the jump from waitressing in Kansas City to standing up her own pottery business, The Object Enthusiast. In Reinhardt's case, the up-front investment hadn't come from a bank, or even from an artistically minded nonprofit or philanthropist. It came from a former professor, a mentor from her student days at Kansas State University, who had chosen simply to gift her his old equipment. Over the course of the following years, Reinhardt managed to build The Object Enthusiast into a very successful venture, eventually earning a fairly comfortable living. Demand began to outstrip her ability to supply new pieces on a timely basis. To keep her customers satisfied, she needed to expand, to find a larger space, and to hire a colleague to share in the work. The question was where she would get the money to make the jump.

Enter AltCap. In 2017, the company, which lends very small amounts to entrepreneurs, offered Reinhardt a loan. She used that funding to hire an assistant and move her equipment into a studio with additional production capacity.[57] Suddenly, The Object Enthusiast was pumping out more pottery—and the pieces continued flying off the shelves. The company's revenue doubled in a single year. As Reinhardt later concluded, "For somebody in the beginning stages of making something come to life, a gift or microloan could be huge."[58] Her story demonstrates clearly how access to a bit of capital can make or break a successful business.

Not every would-be entrepreneur will be as successful as Emily Reinhardt. Not everyone who dreams of establishing their own company will get $5,000 worth of equipment and a *huge* boost of confidence from a mentor at the beginning of their journey. But ask yourself: How many Americans work today in jobs that they do not find fulfilling? How many spend hours each day dreaming of making a go of their own business? How many are convinced that they could successfully provide a new product or service? We'll hazard to guess that there are *millions*. But Democrats rarely speak to their dreams, let alone their frustrations.

For too long, Democrats have stood silent as Republicans styled themselves as the party of "the job creators," suggesting, however implicitly, that we're merely the party of the job *fillers*. Democrats need to demonstrate that they *also* believe in free enterprise. We need to convince voters that we are equipped to become beacons of an economic agenda that celebrates those taking the risks required to grow the economy. By fueling an explosion of new entrepreneurship, Democrats will not only be the party championing equality—we'll be the party of opportunity as well. By crafting smart solutions and then marketing them to entrepreneurs and founders in both red *and* blue America, Opportunity Democrats have a clear opening to make good on the promise of their creed.

BEYOND THE REBOUND

Virginia's Seventh Congressional District isn't designed to be won on the margins. Encompassing several suburbs outside Richmond and a portion of the commonwealth's rural countryside, the district is 70 percent white.[1] Republicans won the seat in the early 1970s and held it for decades. After winning the seat in 2001, Representative Eric Cantor emerged as a GOP star, rising to become House Majority Leader. In 2012, Virginia remapped the border of his district to make it even more reliably conservative—a move that backfired when Cantor lost a primary race to a Tea Party firebrand named Dave Brat in 2014. Many figured the district was destined to be represented by conservatives forever.

But then came Abigail Spanberger.

Spanberger had grown up in a portion of the Seventh District. Early in her career, she served the nation as an officer in the CIA. She was, and is, more moderate than most Democrats representing liberal bastions like New York or San Francisco. But she believes in the foundation of the Democratic agenda—in preserving the Affordable Care Act, in LGBT rights, in a woman's right to choose. More than that, she believes that expanding opportunity is more important than fanning the ideological outrage that so frequently consumes the nation's political dialogue. Believing that Dave Brat was out of step with his admittedly conservative constituents, she decided to challenge him in the 2018 election—as a Democrat.

Spanberger made an important choice in her campaign. She refused to let her messaging be sucked into debates about President Trump. She wasn't going to spend her time bashing him or shaming his supporters. Rather, as she put it, her campaign "focused on the needs of the people, the voters. We talked about the substantive issues affecting their lives, we stood up for American values, and we brought respect and decency back to the political process."[2] And here's what's important for Opportunity Democrats: she won. She won in a district that favors Republicans. And her victory helped propel Democrats back into the House majority.

Spanberger's victory didn't emerge in a vacuum. Brat was unpopular, having proven himself to be more of a show horse than a work horse in Washington. By the fall of 2018, President Trump had worn out his welcome among suburban voters, many of whom were disgusted by his draconian approach to children suffering at the nation's southern border. Spanberger benefited, in other words, from "the rebound." Some voters who had supported Brat two years earlier—or had chosen not to vote in the 2016 election—cast ballots for her simply to send a message to President Trump.

But there are two things about that. First, the rebound wouldn't have boosted just *any* Democratic candidate to victory in that part of Virginia. Our party could not have run the sort of candidate poised to win in the bluest of blue districts and still beaten Brat. Spanberger offered a thoughtful, common sense policy agenda centered on *opportunity* throughout her campaign. And that, combined with a biography that burnished her credentials as a service-oriented pragmatist, made her a viable alternative to Brat's archconservatism.

Second, and probably more important, Spanberger's strategy was designed explicitly to appeal to voters regardless of what they think of Trump or the GOP in general. She was elected (and has since governed) not on an agenda that responds reflexively as the antithesis of conservative nationalism. Rather, she legislates as an Opportunity Democrat, readily aware that pragmatism is the only way she'll continue winning over the swing voters and others who might otherwise vote for her opponent (or stay home) in subsequent contests.

In 2019, two Democratic gubernatorial candidates used much the same approach to prevail in states that Trump won handily in 2016. Andy Beshear was elected governor of Kentucky and John Bel Edwards was reelected governor of Louisiana explicitly because they refused to let far-left ideological politics overwhelm the messages they wanted to communicate about how they intended to govern. As they wrote together after their victories, "To win, we had to reach out to people across the political spectrum, including people who voted for President Trump…We urge Democrats to focus on, care about and invest more in state races, and to look at our victories as blueprints for how to win across the country."[3]

Democrats can't let their agenda be hijacked by the GOP. By

becoming nothing but a party bent on "resisting" President Trump's agenda, we let Republicans set the table. If we're simply the "no" to their "yes," we allow them to define the landscape of ideas. If our talking points are suffocated by a conversation almost exclusively about whatever it is that President Trump (or whoever succeeds him) is tweeting, we lose our voice. And we can't let that happen.

We believe Spanberger, Beshear, and Edwards know what they're talking about and, if nothing else, this book was written to help amplify their message. Our party can't be held captive by the GOP's efforts to define us any more than we can hope that the same ideas and script that have defined Democrats for decades will suddenly empower us to prevail. Democrats need to have an affirmative point of view that exists *irrespective* of what our adversaries believe. We need our candidates and ideas to appeal independently to a sufficiently large swath of the electorate to sustain a governing majority over the long term.

A few months before a resounding set of victories for Democrats in the 2018 midterms, one political analyst wrote: "A year and a half after the most bigoted, misogynistic, jingoistic president in living memory won the election and polluted the political culture, Democratic leaders are still just letting him talk because they aren't clear what they have to say for themselves."[4] We need a message and platform that doesn't depend so heavily on people wanting to reject Trump. The Opportunity Agenda is our attempt to point the way forward.

HOW DEMOCRATS WIN

Many of the ideas that we've endorsed in the preceding chapters may seem, at first blush, uncontroversial. Who would oppose improving schools and colleges, or updating the way we construct the social safety net for the twenty-first century, or expanding access to capital? And on some level, that's by design. Taking the advice offered by Democrats who have won in red states and districts, when putting together these first building blocks of the Opportunity Agenda, we scanned the policy horizon for issues that met three criteria.

First, each element needs to address voters' bread-and-butter concerns. They may *not* be hot buttons on Twitter, but they need to be relevant to the discussions voters have at the kitchen table. People worry about their children's futures every day. They fret over their retirement. They're concerned about how an economic downturn might affect their family's bottom line. The Opportunity Agenda needs to make clear to voters that our party is equipped to address those concerns.

Second, these ideas aren't entirely new to the Democratic lexicon—they're just too frequently relegated to the second and third tiers of our broader agenda. To the degree that only a select sliver of American voters focus on more than a handful of policy specifics before selecting their candidate, the topics we've chosen are something akin to the fine print included in a long, convoluted contract. The electorate will develop its impression of the Democratic agenda by metabolizing the limited number of issues we crow about most frequently. We doubt many Democrats will take much issue with many of these proposals—though some inevitably will. We simply believe they deserve top billing in a way they have never before received.

Third, these ideas are designed explicitly to signal to voters outside our base that they can be comfortable joining our cause. We know that, to win, Democrats must do more than make sure every committed liberal gets to the polls on every Election Day. We need to build bridges to communities that require persuasion, and who, as we like to say among ourselves, are "at risk" for voting for the GOP. The Opportunity Agenda is a policy platform written to expand our party's appeal.

Not all Democratic strategists will accede that this is the right approach. Some may see greater wisdom in making the differences between Democrats and Republicans starker.[5] In some cases, that may be driven by (entirely legitimate) disgust with Trump's agenda. And we don't doubt that there are reasons to believe that the Democratic Party's most promising road to success is predicated on whipping up the public's frustration with the GOP. Our point is simple: anger may be enough to beat Trump in 2020 (though we can't be sure of even that), but if we intend to win over the long term and build a sustainable majority, we need a more comprehensive approach. In the wake of Trump's disastrous presidency, it's natural to feel angry. But we think Democrats need to prioritize getting even.

Some may accuse us of offering weak tea—of failing to meet the divisiveness of the Trump agenda with a Democrat agenda that's equally controversial. If Twitter is the primary lens you use to understand the world of politics, you may be tempted to believe that the most divisive Democratic ideas are best equipped to drive our victory because, well, they're good at stirring the pot.[6] But Democrats shouldn't be proposing ideas that stir up our base or simply stick it to our ideological opponents. We should be standing up for ideas that expand our appeal to portions of the electorate that aren't exactly sure whether they'll vote in subsequent elections—or, if they do, who they'll vote for.

Studies bear this point out. Using data derived by the Hidden Tribes project, the *New York Times* concluded in 2019, "The outspoken group of Democratic-leaning voters on social media is outnumbered, roughly 2 to 1, by the more moderate, more diverse and less educated group of Democrats who typically don't post political content online." Only a tenth of self-described Democrats view themselves as "socialist." Only one in four are "ideologically aligned" progressives.[7] So, for all the impression that there's political benefit to embracing a more explicitly radical agenda, the reality is that Democrats thrive when their ideas appeal across a much wider spectrum. *That's* the key to overcoming the limits of any rebound strategy.

The stakes are just too high for us to allow our emotions to get the best of our strategic direction. *New York Times* columnist David Leonhardt made exactly this point in a column following one of the early 2020 presidential debates:

> You would think that Democrats would be approaching the 2020 campaign with a ruthless sense of purpose. But they're not, at least not yet. They are not focusing on issues that expose Trump's many vulnerabilities. They have instead devoted substantial time to wonky subjects that excite some progressive activists—and alienate most American voters.[8]

It's not that we shouldn't be angered by the Trump agenda. It's that we need to harness that anger for something productive. The Opportunity Agenda gives us a way to do exactly that.

A STRATEGY *FOR YOU*

What, in the end, is the Opportunity Agenda? We've made some suggestions in the preceding pages, but the ideas laid out in the book aren't meant to be exhaustive. At root, we simply believe that, in every possible way and at every possible moment, Democrats need to be making the case for what exactly we will do *for you*. We need to highlight the benefits we are going to provide directly *for you and your family*. What value proposition are we offering? What problems will we solve if you elect us to office? Our commitments to social justice and economic equality are important. But when we're talking to voters, we need to explain exactly what we intend to do *for them*.

We're convinced that breaking our dependence on the rebound begins with ideas. And we hope our party continually scans the horizon for ideas to add—proposals that will ensure that life is better *for you*.

Take one example: we believe Democrats would do well to develop a new clarion call for national service. If this marks the most fevered political moment in the nation's history since Vietnam, a new national service program holds the potential to reweave the American fabric. This isn't a new idea per se—national service has been a staple of Democratic campaign platforms since the 1960s. But the call to serve, whether in the military or a civilian capacity, is almost an afterthought today, paid lip service by various candidates (or written into the Democratic National Platform) without becoming the focus of any outreach to voters.

Service programs have taken different forms through the years. President Kennedy championed the Peace Corps. President Clinton fought to pass AmeriCorps. Today, Hartford has created a new and very successful Youth Service Corps.[9] The challenge now is to imagine how to shape and scale service programs that work in the twenty-first century. Instead of free college for all, should the government provide two years of college tuition in exchange for two years of service? Or two years of trade school? Beyond providing for new entitlements, how do we make service, once again, a cornerstone of the American social contract?

Opportunity Democrats should be burnishing a sense among the public that we're committed to bringing the country together in a moment of dispiriting political turmoil. We need to be nimble, finding issues that speak to our general orientation—namely that Democrats are poised to work *for you*—when they arise on national, state, and city levels. But it can't end there. We can't rely simply on the hope that the policy ideas we propose will change the way the public perceives our party. We can't just hope that our most talented messaging mavens will discipline our candidates so our Opportunity Agenda emerges as our party's calling card in every community. Rather, we need to develop a narrative that replaces the public perception that left Democrats vulnerable to Donald Trump's attacks in the 2016 election.

To get there, Opportunity Democrats need to invest in the tools that have helped Republicans build their brand at the state and local level. Take, as one example, the American Legislative Exchange Council (ALEC), a well-financed advocacy group that plies conservative state and local elected officials with policy ideas that they can champion in their respective legislatures. Set aside the widespread accusations that ALEC is simply a foil for special interests to funnel contributions to conservative legislators—let's emulate what ALEC does effectively.[10] Opportunity Democrats should scale and develop additional organizations that spread good ideas and best practices among legislators who share our values and outlook.

Second, Opportunity Democrats need to be strategic about how we collect and distribute resources among our allies. We should be developing networks of support, cognizant of the fact that an emerging Opportunity Democrat working on a local level today can quickly become an important figure at the state or federal level tomorrow. Conservatives have made an art of mutual support—we ought to learn from their success.

Third, we need to build up our grassroots. Today, much like with social media, the most vocal activists in any given community are likely to be the most politically polarized. For that reason, issues that may not be foremost concerns for many Opportunity Democrats become flashpoints on Twitter—and they frequently dominate any given news cycle. By contrast, citizens focused more exclusively on *our* priorities—improving education, growing the economy, enhancing the nation's infrastructure—are often less likely to engage. That need not be the case. More of us need to attend town hall meetings, send messages to legislators, and organize protests of our own. In a world where *everyone* is busy, even a little bit of grassroots support can go a long way.

In that same vein, we shouldn't just encourage committed Opportunity Democrats to get more involved—we should be recruiting our friends, neighbors, and acquaintances to join our various causes, and most importantly, to *vote*. Every state and locality can be improved by ideas born out of the values embodied in our creed. And too often our fear of offending someone spurs us to demur in asking them to join our cause. That's a mistake. We can be proud of our ideas—and we should invite others to join us in our mission. As President Obama said in his first presidential campaign, "We are the change that we seek." That's as true today as it was then—and it's as true at the state and local levels as it is in Washington. Get involved, support your fellow Opportunity Democrats, and spread the gospel that holds the best hope for building a society that's safe, secure, and prosperous in the twenty-first century.

HOPE FOR THE FUTURE

In the wake of President Trump's election, a new generation of citizens, many of whom might otherwise have sat on the sidelines, decided to get more involved in American politics. They registered to vote. They volunteered on campaigns. And in many cases, they chose to run for office themselves. This newly awakened generation of activists reflected the great, broad diversity of the Democratic Party. In April 2018, 424 women had filed to run for House seats—a record.[11] And at the state level, one Democratic group reported an 87 percent spike in applications to run for office just months after Trump's inauguration.[12]

Some of that surge is due to pure enthusiasm—millennials were overdue for a political awakening, and they may well spark change throughout the nation's political system. But the new excitement is also due in large part to the work of advocacy groups who are inspiring, recruiting, and training individuals who might never otherwise have chosen public office. Organizations like EMILY's List and Run for Something are cultivating a legion of new Democrats who, we hope, will spend years accruing power and fighting to help those who need a hand up.

But sustaining this push won't happen on its own. Trump won't always be there to scare voters into supporting our candidates.

Beyond whatever muscle we put into this new generation of Democratic public servants—money, time, attention—ultimately, their success will rest on the strength of their ideas. Will they offer solutions to the twenty-first century challenges that face the population at large? Will they solve for the nation's sputtering education system? Will they reweave the safety net to catch those who might otherwise fall through? Will they make the investments necessary to fuel economic growth? Will they build an ecosystem where everyone has an opportunity to make the most of their talents?

In this book, we've outlined a playbook designed to drive the Democratic Party forward. But our ideas will only succeed if the grassroots embrace them, champion them, and drive the nation's leaders to turn them into law. We need citizens of every stripe to get involved. To support Opportunity Democrats. To volunteer for their campaigns. To tout them on social media. And to run for office when there's a need and an opportunity.

We believe America's future is promising. We believe the twenty-first century can be defined by American prosperity. But to get there, we need to drive change, both within the Democratic Party and across the country. The Opportunity Agenda is, in our view, an important part of the way forward. We intend to put it at the heart of our work. We hope you will join us in our mission.

ACKNOWLEDGMENTS

The Opportunity Agenda would not have been possible without the hard work and determination of so many people. While there are far too many people who have influenced my life and the writing of this book to list, there are a few who must be recognized for their dedication to this enormous undertaking.

First and foremost, this never would have been possible without my friend and coauthor, Mayor Sly James. When I first met Sly a few years ago, I was immediately impressed with the clarity of his convictions, his commitment to public service and improving the lives of all people, and, of course, his incredible sense of humor, which came in handy during some intense working sessions over BBQ in Kansas City. I'm eternally grateful that he embarked on this project with me.

To Marty Edelman, my mentor, second father, and lifelong friend who has helped me achieve so much both personally and professionally. Without his guidance and sage wisdom, I don't know where I'd be. I'm blessed to have him in my life.

Producing *The Opportunity Agenda* required the support of many in order to guide the book from a concept to the finished product. I'm grateful for my chief of staff, Brad Katz; Joni Wickham from Wickham James; and the team from Global Strategy Group: Jon Silvan, Justin Lapatine, Tim Roberts, Jason Green, and Will Warren-O'Brien. You spent countless hours helping research, review, and rereview this book, and I appreciate all your hard work.

I want to thank Naren Aryal and Kristin Perry from Amplify Publishing and Dan Gerstein from Gotham Ghostwriters. Your guidance was essential for this rookie who had never written a book. You made this process both simple and seamless.

A special thank you goes out to Marc Dunkelman who helped Sly and me take our (sometimes scattered!) ideas and turn them into persuasive prose. I'm sure we were quite a handful to deal with at times, and you did an amazing job.

Finally, many of the policy ideas and personal stories included in *The Opportunity Agenda* came from friends serving in public office and running well-regarded organizations. I'd like to specifically thank Congresswomen Abigail Spanberger and Chrissy Houlahan, Oregon State Treasurer Tobias Read, Jukay Hsu from Pursuit, Jonathan Bowles and Eli Dvorkin from the Center for an Urban Future, and the entire team at Third Way.

—WINSTON FISHER

The Opportunity Agenda is about how the Democratic Party can improve outcomes for the middle class by reexamining policy and assumptions. This book examines foundational economic and equity issues and suggests plausible, pragmatic responses that we believe the Democratic Party should adopt and champion.

Winston Fisher brought me into this project. He traveled to Kansas City, Missouri, from New York City and sat in my office for a couple hours to talk politics—what we thought of the present and how we might reenvision the future. There was no talk of a book project during that initial meeting, just a couple of guys from different paths exploring shared goals and ideals. What started as a conversation between the two of us became a collaboration on a book project about all of us.

Talking ideas is easy. Making those ideas worthy of serious public consideration is a much more difficult and painstaking endeavor. We were fortunate enough to have a small army helping us with this book to organize the facts, data, and evidence necessary to bring substance to theory. We sat together for hours over a year and a half arguing points, sharpening ideas, and testing points of view. This cadre kept the project moving and on time. The research and organization were first-rate, and the writing process was superb.

When I was an active trial lawyer, I learned to seek out and rely on experts to do those things I had no business doing. Our team of experts in this process was exceptional. Bradley Katz, Tim Roberts, Justin Lapatine, Will Warren-O'Brien, Jason Green, and Kristin Perry were tireless in their efforts to keep this project moving forward. Marc Dunkelman, who helped us actually write the book, was as patient as a saint. It is only through this true collaborative effort of professionals, who also became friends, that we have been able to produce a product of which we are all proud.

Winston and I agreed that we needed to engage in storytelling in order to illuminate our central goal of creating a bold Democratic plan that will be of benefit to all people. We were very fortunate to find a number of individuals who were willing to share their personal stories, insights, and views with us. Without the voices of those we want to serve, we would have less of a story and more of a scholarly treatise. We are deeply indebted to them for allowing us into their lives.

I am personally blessed to have the constant and liberating support of my wife, Licia, and my children, Malik, Kyle, and Aja, all of whom freely shared their thoughts and ideas about the issues discussed in this work. I am also blessed to have the benefit of keen insights and thoughts of my former chief of staff, current business partner, and author in her own right, Joni Wickham.

Finally, I have great gratitude for my friend and coauthor, Winston Fisher, who brought me into this entire endeavor. Of all those with whom he could have chosen to work, for some odd reason, he chose me. I am forever grateful for his faith and the hard work and dedication of all who have worked tirelessly to turn thoughts into pragmatic approaches that can benefit us all.

—SLY JAMES

ABOUT THE
AUTHORS

WINSTON FISHER

Winston C. Fisher is a partner at Fisher Brothers, a 100-year-old real estate firm based in New York City, where he directs the company's financing and investing activities, property acquisitions and dispositions, and oversees all new development initiatives. He also serves as CEO of AREA15, a first-of-its-kind experiential retail and entertainment company.

Mr. Fisher is a fierce advocate for policies that strengthen New York City and State, serving as cochair of Governor Cuomo's New York City Regional Economic Development Council and on the board of several leading civic institutions, including the Partnership for New York City, the Citizens Budget Commission, the Regional Plan Association, and the Real Estate Board of New York.

A firm believer in the value of providing opportunities for Americans to earn a good life, Mr. Fisher created the Middle Class Jobs Project in 2015 in collaboration with the Center for an Urban Future, a nonpartisan policy organization working to grow the economy in New York City. The project examines a wide range of challenges facing middle-class job growth in New York and identifies practical, implementable solutions elected officials can explore to help expand middle-class job opportunities. The project has produced several full-length policy reports and data briefs and hosted symposiums focused on creating economic opportunities for New Yorkers to enter the middle class in a digital economy. A number of the project's key recommendations have influenced policy at the state and local level.

In 2018 and 2019, Mr. Fisher partnered with Third Way, a national think tank, to organize strategy sessions in Columbus, Ohio, and Charleston, South Carolina. The strategy sessions brought together several hundred leading Democrats from across the country to shape and advance a new economic and electoral conversation.

Involved in a number of philanthropic activities, Mr. Fisher is the executive vice chairman of the Fisher House Foundation, a national not-for-profit established to support and house injured armed services veterans and their families, and he is on the board of the Intrepid Sea, Air & Space Museum. He holds a bachelor of arts in philosophy from Syracuse University, class of '96.

SLY JAMES

Sly James is the former mayor of Kansas City, Missouri, and responsible for overseeing the city's renaissance. Throughout his tenure, he moved the needle on universal pre-K, spearheaded the construction and expansion of a transformative streetcar line, and successfully passed an $800 million infrastructure package that created the first "Smart City" initiative in North America. Benefits of this initiative included: attracting an 800-room convention hotel to the heart of Kansas City's downtown, collaborating with Major League Baseball and the Royals to build the Kansas City Urban Youth Academy, and closing the gap between the city's third grade reading proficiency and the state average by a third.

Additionally, Mr. James was translating his commitment to diversity into action long before today's momentum around equity began to take shape. As president of the Kansas City Metropolitan Bar Association (KCMBA) in 2003, he organized the managing partners of the largest firms in the city to form the Diversity Initiative, which remains a well-respected and meaningful activity of the KCMBA today.

Mr. James won numerous awards while mayor, including public television's American Graduate Champion of Education, Visit KC Tourism Icon Award, Kansas City Area Development Council One KC Award, Paid Leave Leader from the National Partnership for Children and Families, and Government Technology's Top 25 Doers, Dreamers and Drivers. He has also worked with various organizations in leadership positions, including the African American Mayors Association, National Democratic Mayors, the Missouri Board of Law Examiners, and Economic Development Corporation. Mr. James was also a visiting fellow at the Harvard

Institute of Politics in 2015 and participated in a number of White House initiatives addressing transportation, crime, workforce development, and others.

After serving as a military police officer in the Marines from 1971 to 1975 in California, the Philippines, and Japan during the Vietnam War, Mr. James graduated cum laude from Rockhurst College with a bachelor of arts in English. He then went on to earn his law degree, also cum laude, from the University of Minnesota in 1983. Prior to his election, he enjoyed a successful legal career that spanned almost three decades.

ENDNOTES

INTRODUCTION: COMPELLING ANSWERS *FOR YOU*

1   Twitter Inc. "Ctr for Urban Future @Nycfuture." Periscope. https://www.pscp.
    tv/w/1mrGmYDkdmMGy.

2   Julian Wylie, "Life Expectancy Down in US Compared to Other Countries,"
    AARP, September 21, 2018, https://www.aarp.org/health/healthy-living/
    info-2018/life-expectancy-down.html.

3   Doug Newcomb, "Transportation Secretary Foxx On Why Columbus, Ohio
    Won The DOT's $40 Million Smart City Challenge," *Forbes*, June 24, 2016,
    https://www.forbes.com/sites/dougnewcomb/2016/06/24/transportation-
    secretary-foxx-on-why-columbus-ohio-won-the-dots-40-million-smart-
    city-challenge/#3a75b18045db.

4   Pete Bigelow, "The Future of Transportation: Q&A with DOT Secretary
    Anthony Foxx," *Car and Driver*, October 24, 2016, https://www.
    caranddriver.com/news/a15344491/future-of-transportation-qa-with-dot-
    secretary-anthony-foxx/.

CHAPTER 1: THE MOST IMPORTANT YEARS OF OUR LIVES

1   "Indiana Election Results 2016: President Live Map by County, Real-Time Voting Updates," *POLITICO*, https://www.politico.com/2016-election/results/map/president/indiana/.

2   Mark Michelson, "LSC Communications Expanding Mattoon Facility, Closing Gallatin Plant," *Printing Impressions*, January 31, 2017, https://www.piworld.com/article/lsc-communications-expanding-mattoon-facility-closing-gallatin-plant/.

3   "Indiana Economy at a Glance," US Bureau of Labor Statistics, https://www.bls.gov/eag/eag.in.htm#eag_in.f.2.

4   Jim Johnson, "Study: Local Economy Suffering from Child Care Needs in Indiana Counties," *Indiana Economic Digest*, https://indianaeconomicdigest.com/Content/Most-Recent/Parke/Article/Study-Local-economy-suffering-from-child-care-needs-in-Indiana-counties/31/214/93989.

5   Jeanie Lindsay, "In Perry County, Workforce Needs Drive Expansion to Childcare, Preschool Access." *Indiana Public Media*, https://indianapublicmedia.org/news/in-perry-county,-workforce-needs-drive-expansion-to-childcare,-preschool-access.php.

6   Jim Johnson, "Study: Local Economy Suffering from Child Care Needs in Indiana Counties," *Indiana Economic Digest*, https://indianaeconomicdigest.com/Content/Most-Recent/Parke/Article/Study-Local-economy-suffering-from-child-care-needs-in-Indiana-counties/31/214/93989.

7   "ConnectingVets, 05/18/18—How Chrissy Houlahan Transitioned from a Life of Military Service to Civic Service," Chrissy for Congress, June 22, 2018, https://www.chrissyhoulahanforcongress.com/news/2018/6/22/connectingvets-051818-how-chrissy-houlahan-transitioned-from-a-life-of-military-service-to-civic-service.

8   Tom Bowman, "To Retain More Parents, The Military Offers A Better Work-Life Balance," NPR, October 12, 2016, https://www.npr.org/sections/parallels/2016/10/12/496911192/to-retain-more-women-the-military-offers-a-better-work-life-balance.

9   "How Working Parents Share Parenting and Household Responsibilities," Pew Research Center's Social & Demographic Trends Project, December 31, 2019, https://www.pewsocialtrends.org/2015/11/04/raising-kids-and-running-a-household-how-working-parents-share-the-load/.

10 "Facts Over Time—Women in Labor Force," Women's Bureau, US Department of Labor, https://www.dol.gov/agencies/wb/data/facts-over-time

11 Lynn A. Karoly and Anamarie A. Whitaker, "Informing Investments in Preschool Quality and Access in Cincinnati: Evidence of Impacts and Economic Returns from National, State, and Local Preschool Programs," RAND Corporation, March 11, 2016, https://www.rand.org/pubs/research_reports/RR1461.html.

12 "GEEARS Fact Sheet," Georgia Early Education Alliance for Ready Students, May 2011, http://geears.org/wp-content/uploads/2011/05/GEEARSFactSheet.pdf.

13 Ibid.

14 Joe Pinsker, "Parenting Like an Economist Is a Lot Less Stressful," *The Atlantic*, April 23, 2019, https://www.theatlantic.com/family/archive/2019/04/oster-cribsheet-parenting-guide/587734/.

15 Clem Richardson, "Harlem Children's Zone's Baby College Teaches Local Parents How to Best Raise Their Children from the Start," *New York Daily News*, January 10, 2019, https://www.nydailynews.com/new-york/harlem-children-zone-baby-college-teaches-local-parents-best-raise-children-start-article-1.1019190.

16 "The Baby College," Harlem Children's Zone, https://hcz.org/our-programs/the-baby-college/.

17 Clem Richardson, "Harlem Children's Zone's Baby College Teaches Local Parents How to Best Raise Their Children from the Start," *New York Daily News*, January 10, 2019, https://www.nydailynews.com/new-york/harlem-children-zone-baby-college-teaches-local-parents-best-raise-children-start-article-1.1019190.

18 Lauren Lee, "Jennifer Garner Teams up with Save the Children to Fight Rural Poverty in America," CNN, February 26, 2019, https://www.cnn.com/2018/07/23/us/iyw-save-the-children-rural-childhood-poverty/index.html.

19 Valerie Strauss, "Jennifer Garner Urges Congress to Fund Early-Childhood Education: 'A Brain in Poverty Is up against It. I'm Telling You,'" *Washington Post*, April 18, 2019, https://www.washingtonpost.com/news/answer-sheet/wp/2017/03/16/jennifer-garner-urges-congress-to-fund-early-childhood-education-a-brain-in-poverty-is-up-against-it-im-telling-you/.

20 Chris Morran, "Should Hospitals Stop Giving Out Free Samples of Baby Formula to New Moms?" *Consumerist*, April 9, 2012, https://consumerist.com/2012/04/should-hospitals-stop-giving-out-free-samples-of-baby-formula-to-new-moms.html.

21 Ibid.

22 "Family and Medical Leave (FMLA)," US Department of Labor, https://www.dol.gov/general/topic/benefits-leave/fmla.

23 "Toxic Stress," Center on the Developing Child at Harvard University, https://developingchild.harvard.edu/science/key-concepts/toxic-stress/.

24 "LINC-UP," Early Childhood-LINC / The Center for the Study of Social Policy, Issue 35, October 2017.

25 "About," Providence Talks, http://www.providencetalks.org/about/.

26 "Parents," Providence Talks, http://www.providencetalks.org/parents/.

27 Ibid.

28 "Providence—2013 Mayors Challenge Grand Prize Winner," Mayors Challenge, https://mayorschallenge.bloomberg.org/ideas/providence-talks/.

29 "LENA: Building Brains Through Early Talk," LENA, http://www.lena.org/.

30 "U.S. Census Bureau QuickFacts: Kansas City City, Missouri," Census Bureau QuickFacts, https://www.census.gov/quickfacts/kansascitycitymissouri.

31 Bria Anderson, interview by authors, phone, October 14, 2019.

32 Bruce Atchison et al., "Trends in Pre-K Education Funding in 2017-18," Education Commission of the States, February 2019, https://www.ecs.org/trends-in-pre-k-education-funding-in-2017-18/.

33 Eliza Shapiro, "Bright Spot for N.Y.'s Struggling Schools: Pre-K," *New York Times*, January 1, 2019. https://www.nytimes.com/2019/01/01/nyregion/deblasio-pre-k-program-nyc.html.

34 Ben Chapman, "EXCLUSIVE: Mayor De Blasio's Pre-Kindergarten Expansion Caused Public School Overcrowding, Report Says," *New York Daily News*, December 20, 2018, https://www.nydailynews.com/new-york/education/ny-metro-de-blasio-prek-led-to-school-overcrowding-20181217-story.html.

35 Eileen Appelbaum, Heather Boushey, and John Schmitt, "The Economic Importance of Women's Rising Hours of Work," Center for American Progress, April 2014, https://cdn.americanprogress.org/wp-content/uploads/2014/04/WomensRisingWorkv2.pdf.

36 Rasheed Malik, "The Effects of Universal Preschool in Washington,
    D.C.," Center for American Progress, September 26, 2018, https://www.
    americanprogress.org/issues/early-childhood/reports/2018/09/26/458208/
    effects-universal-preschool-washington-d-c/.

37 Bryce Covert, "How Universal Free Preschool in DC Helped Bring
    Moms Back to Work," *Vox*, September 26, 2018, https://www.vox.
    com/identities/2018/9/26/17902864/preschool-benefits-working-
    mothers-parents.

38 Laure Littlepage, "Lost Opportunities: The Impact of Inadequate Child Care
    on Indiana's Workforce & Economy," Issue 18-C16, Early Learning Indiana,
    June 2018, https://earlylearningin.org/wp-content/uploads/2018/10/
    economic.impact_early.learning_sep.28.2018_final.pdf.

39 Megan Feldman, "New Report Highlights How Child Care Challenges Affect
    Georgia's Workforce and Economy," First Five Years Fund, November
    1, 2018, https://www.ffyf.org/new-report-highlights-how-child-care-
    challenges-affect-georgias-workforce-and-economy/.

40 Richard Chase et al., "The Economic Impacts of the Child Care Shortage
    in Northeastern Minnesota," Northland Foundation, July 2018, https://
    northlandfdn.org/news/publications/childcare-shortage-report-2018.pdf.

41 Rebecca Linke, "Child Care Is So Expensive I Can't Afford to
    Work," *Cognoscenti*, August 21, 2018, https://www.wbur.org/
    cognoscenti/2018/08/21/the-cost-of-being-a-working-parent-rebecca-linke.

42 Kristen Doerer, "How Much Does It Cost to Leave the Workforce to Care
    for a Child? A Lot More Than You Think," PBS, June 21, 2016, https://
    www.pbs.org/newshour/economy/how-much-does-it-cost-to-leave-the-
    workforce-to-care-for-a-child-a-lot-more-than-you-think.

43 Matt Campbell, "With New Bridge across Troost, Operation Breakthrough
    to Expand, Serve Hundreds More," *The Kansas City Star*, February 22, 2018,
    https://www.kansascity.com/news/local/article201594649.html.

44 Leah Wankum, "Operation Breakthrough Expansion Gives Every Child a
    Chance, Mayor Says," *Startland News*, February 28, 2018, https://www.
    startlandnews.com/2018/02/operation-breakthrough-expansion/.

45 "Quality Early Childhood Education: Lifelong Gains," First Five Years Fund,
    https://www.ffyf.org/why-it-matters/lifelong-gains/.

46 Libby Nelson, "The Big Benefit of Pre-K Might Not Be Education," *Vox*, July
    30, 2014, https://www.vox.com/2014/7/30/5952739/the-research-on-how-
    pre-k-could-reduce-crime.

47 Camille Phillips, "Report: Students in Pre-K 4 SA Scored Better on State
    Tests, Missed Fewer Days of School," Texas Public Radio, January 29, 2019,
    https://www.tpr.org/post/report-students-pre-k-4-sa-scored-better-state-
    tests-missed-fewer-days-school.

48 "The Current State of Scientific Knowledge on Pre-Kindergarten Effects,"
    April 4, 2017, https://www.brookings.edu/wp-content/uploads/2017/04/
    duke_prekstudy_final_4-4-17_hires.pdf.

49 Donald J. Hernandez, "Double Jeopardy: How Third-Grade Reading Skills
    and Poverty Influence High School Graduation," The Annie E. Casey
    Foundation, April 2011, http://files.eric.ed.gov/fulltext/ED518818.pdf.

50 "Trends in High School Dropout and Completion Rates in the United
    States," National Center for Education Statistics, https://nces.ed.gov/
    programs/dropout/intro.asp.

51 Arthur J. Reynolds et al., "Age 26 Cost-Benefit Analysis of the Child-Parent
    Center Early Education Program," Child Development 82, no. 1 (2011):
    379–404, https://doi.org/10.1111/j.1467-8624.2010.01563.x

52 Libby Nelson, "The Big Benefit of Pre-K Might Not Be Education," Vox, July
    30, 2014, https://www.vox.com/2014/7/30/5952739/the-research-on-how-
    pre-k-could-reduce-crime.

53 Bryce Covert, "How Universal Free Preschool in DC Helped Bring
    Moms Back to Work," Vox, September 26, 2018, https://www.vox.
    com/identities/2018/9/26/17902864/preschool-benefits-working-
    mothers-parents.

CHAPTER 2: A SECOND REVOLUTION IN AMERICAN EDUCATION

1 "A Nation at Risk," US Department of Education, April 1983, https://www2.
   ed.gov/pubs/NatAtRisk/risk.html.

2 Selim Algar and Carl Campanile, "CUNY's Lax Placement Standards
   Yields Fewer Remedial Students," New York Post, July 17, 2018, https://
   nypost.com/2018/07/16/cunys-lax-placement-standards-yields-fewer-
   remedial-students/.

3 Valerie J. Calderon, Frank Newport, and Nate Dvorak, "Confidence in U.S.
   Public Schools Rallies," Gallup, November 18, 2019, https://news.gallup.
   com/poll/219143/confidence-public-schools-rallies.aspx.

4   World Bank, "World Development Report 2019: The Changing Nature of Work," World Bank, 20. doi:10.1596/978-1-4648-1328-3.

5   Ibid, page 18.

6   Lauren Weber, "Why Companies Are Failing at Reskilling," *Wall Street Journal*, April 19, 2019, https://www.wsj.com/articles/the-answer-to-your-companys-hiring-problem-might-be-right-under-your-nose-11555689542.

7   World Bank, "World Development Report 2019: The Changing Nature of Work," World Bank, 3. doi:10.1596/978-1-4648-1328-3.

8   Ibid, page 23.

9   Laura Faith Kebede, "Amid Renewed Focus on Job Training in High School, Memphis Students Consider Their Options," *Chalkbeat*, July 6, 2018, https://tn.chalkbeat.org/2018/7/5/21105307/amid-renewed-focus-on-job-training-in-high-school-memphis-students-consider-their-options.

10 Matt Barnum, "One Big Upside of Career and Tech Programs? They Push More Kids to Graduate," *Chalkbeat*, April 19, 2018, https://www.chalkbeat.org/2018/4/19/21104795/one-big-upside-of-career-and-tech-programs-they-push-more-kids-to-graduate.

11 Laura Faith Kebede, "Workforce Training Programs May Soon Look Different in Memphis Schools." *Chalkbeat*, May 9, 2018, https://tn.chalkbeat.org/2018/2/12/21105011/workforce-training-programs-may-soon-look-different-in-memphis-schools.

12 Ibid.

13 Roy Maurer, "Training People for Jobs to Fill the Skills Gap," SHRM, August 16, 2019, https://www.shrm.org/resourcesandtools/hr-topics/talent-acquisition/pages/training-people-for-jobs-to-solve-the-nations-skills-gap.aspx.

14 Samantha McLaren, "These Industries Will Face the Biggest Talent Shortages by 2030," LinkedIn, July 24, 2018, https://business.linkedin.com/talent-solutions/blog/trends-and-research/2018/industries-biggest-talent-shortages-2030.

15 Andrew Van Dam, "Public-School Salaries Fall Short of Average in Nearly Every State," *Washington Post*, January 30, 2019, https://www.washingtonpost.com/us-policy/2019/01/29/what-industry-has-seen-pay-fall-below-average-most-states-public-schools/.

16 Kate Zernike, "Camden Superintendent Who Led Turnaround Is Stepping Down," *New York Times*, April 11, 2018, https://www.nytimes.com/2018/04/11/nyregion/camden-superintendent-paymon-rouhanifard-resigning.html.

17 "Against All Odds, Camden Schools Make Big Strides: Editorial," NJ.com,
    July 22, 2019, https://www.nj.com/opinion/2019/07/against-all-odds-
    camden-schools-make-big-strides-editorial.html.

18 Eliza Shaprio et al., "How an Unknown Reformer Rescued One of
    America's Most Troubled School Districts," *POLITICO Magazine*, June
    30, 2018, https://www.politico.com/magazine/story/2018/06/30/camden-
    superintendent-education-reform-paymon-rouhanifard-218940.

19 Zernike, "Camden."

20 Valerie Strauss, "Blistering Report Details Abject Dysfunction and Dangerous
    Schools in Providence, R.I.," *Washington Post*, June 26, 2019, https://www.
    washingtonpost.com/education/2019/06/26/blistering-report-details-abject-
    dysfunction-dangerous-schools-providence-ri/.

21 Chris Baylor, "Teachers' Unions May Not Raise Pay—but They Do Bolster
    the Democratic Party," *Washington Post*, May 18, 2018, https://www.
    washingtonpost.com/news/monkey-cage/wp/2018/05/18/teachers-unions-
    may-not-raise-pay-but-they-do-bolster-the-democratic-party/?utm_
    term=.359c62dc29d6.

22 "P-TECH Scholars Head to 'New Collar' Future," IBM, May 29, 2018,
    https://www.ibm.com/thought-leadership/ptech/index.html.

23 Diego Mendoza-Moyers, "P-Tech Program Seeks to Bridge New York's
    Education, Skills Gap," *Times Union*, April 27, 2019, https://www.
    timesunion.com/business/article/P-Tech-program-seeks-to-bridge-New-
    York-s-13796066.php.

24 Stan Shoun, interview by Sly James, phone, October 10, 2019.

25 Rebecca Klein, "These Are the Countries Where Kids Go to School for the
    Longest," *HuffPost*, December 7, 2017, https://www.huffpost.com/entry/
    school-life-expectancy-map_n_5599716.

26 "MA Expanded Learning Time (ELT)," MA Expanded Learning Time
    (ELT)—School Redesign, Massachusetts Department of Elementary,
    http://www.doe.mass.edu/redesign/elt/.

27 Marie Anderson, "Longer School Day Debates," *Education*, September 29,
    2016, https://education.seattlepi.com/longer-school-day-debates-1563.html.

28 Amanda Zhou, "Florida Made Days Longer at Low-Performing Schools.
    It Helped," *Chalkbeat*, April 26, 2019, https://www.chalkbeat.org/posts/
    us/2018/08/16/florida-longer-school-day-study/.

29   David Figlio, Kristian L. Holden, and Umut Ozek, "Do Students Benefit from Longer School Days? Regression Discontinuity Evidence from Florida's Additional Hour of Literacy Instruction," Calder National Center for Analysis of Longitudinal Data in Education Research, August 2018, https://caldercenter.org/sites/default/files/CALDER%20WP%20201-0818-1.pdf.

30   Morgan Lee, "Teacher Salaries, School Funding Boosted in New Mexico," *Las Cruces Sun-News*, April 4, 2019, https://www.lcsun-news.com/story/news/local/new-mexico/2019/04/03/new-mexico-governor-teacher-salaries-school-funding-new-laws/3360890002/.

31   Morgan Lee, "New Mexico Awards Funding to Schools to Extend Learning Time," *Associated Press*, May 18, 2019, https://www.apnews.com/2ef8be370e4e415ea80b24aeb41cd54b.

32   Dillon Mullan and Robert Nott, "An Educational Shift Is on the Horizon in New Mexico," *Santa Fe New Mexican*, April 15, 2019, https://www.santafenewmexican.com/news/education/an-educational-shift-is-on-the-horizon-in-new-mexico/article_2ba37391-497d-53d3-afad-a3a977f882ec.html.

33   Morgan Lee, "New Mexico Awards Funding to Schools to Extend Learning Time," *Associated Press*, May 18, 2019, https://www.apnews.com/2ef8be370e4e415ea80b24aeb41cd54b.

34   Dillon Mullan and Robert Nott, "An Educational Shift Is on the Horizon in New Mexico," *Santa Fe New Mexican*, April 15, 2019, https://www.santafenewmexican.com/news/education/an-educational-shift-is-on-the-horizon-in-new-mexico/article_2ba37391-497d-53d3-afad-a3a977f882ec.html.

35   Ibid.

36   Jessica Bies, "Christina's Union Votes 'Yes' on New Incentives, Longer School Years for Wilmington Teachers," *Delaware News Journal*, September 20, 2018, https://www.delawareonline.com/story/news/education/2018/09/20/new-incentives-longer-school-years-christinas-wilmington-teachers/1368275002/.

37   Pursuit LevelUp, interview by authors, email, February 21, 2020.

38   Jessica Smith, "Syracuse University, JPMorgan Chase Collaboration Opens Path to Political Careers for Veterans," Syracuse University, April 9, 2019, https://news.syr.edu/blog/2019/04/09/syracuse-university-jpmorgan-chase-collaboration-opens-path-to-political-careers-for-veterans/.

39 "SAS and FedEx Institute of Technology Collaborate to Grow Data Analytic Capabilities in the Mid-South Region," SAS, January 16, 2018, https://www.sas.com/en_us/news/press-releases/2018/january/analytics-education-fedex-institute-technology.html.

CHAPTER 3: "FIX THE DAMN ROADS"

1   Mallory Simon and Rachel Clarke, "America's Infrastructure Is Crumbling and These People Are Suffering Because of It," CNN, June 22, 2019, https://www.cnn.com/2019/06/17/us/crumbling-american-infrastructure/index.html.

2   "Fix the Damn Roads," Gretchen Whitmer for Governor, https://www.gretchenwhitmer.com/issues/infrastructure/.

3   Donna Borak, "The US Deficit Topped $1 Trillion. The Year's Not Even Over Yet," CNN, September 12, 2019, https://www.cnn.com/2019/09/12/business/us-federal-deficit-august/index.html.

4   Jeff Greenfield et al., "The Ugly History of Stephen Miller's 'Cosmopolitan' Epithet," POLITICO Magazine, August 3, 2017, https://www.politico.com/magazine/story/2017/08/03/the-ugly-history-of-stephen-millers-cosmopolitan-epithet-215454.

5   Samantha Raphelson, "Report Finds More Than 47,000 'Structurally Deficient' Bridges In The U.S.," NPR, April 5, 2019, https://www.npr.org/2019/04/05/710364158/report-finds-more-than-47-000-structurally-deficient-bridges-in-the-u-s.

6   Dina Gusovsky, "America's Water Crisis Goes beyond Flint, Michigan," CNBC, March 28, 2016, https://www.cnbc.com/2016/03/24/americas-water-crisis-goes-beyond-flint-michigan.html.

7   John Hendel and Tucker Doherty, "GRAPHIC: America's Digital Divide, in 2 Maps," POLITICO, February 7, 2018, https://www.politico.com/agenda/story/2018/02/07/digital-divide-in-america-graphic-000639.

8   Ed Mortimer, "Our Crumbling Infrastructure Is Failing Small Businesses," The Hill, March 24, 2019, https://thehill.com/opinion/finance/435344-our-crumbling-infrastructure-is-failing-small-businesses.

9   "The World, Built by China," New York Times, November 18, 2018, https://www.nytimes.com/interactive/2018/11/18/world/asia/world-built-by-china.html.

10 Emma Charlton, "China Is Building 8 New Airports Every Year," World Economic Forum, August 2018, https://www.weforum.org/agenda/2018/08/these-five-charts-show-how-rapidly-china-s-aviation-industry-is-expanding/.

11 Elena Holodny, "The 11 Countries with the Best Infrastructure around the World," *Business Insider*, October 2, 2015, https://www.businessinsider.com/wef-countries-best-infrastructure-world-2015-9#2-singapore-10.

12 Hiba Baroud, "Measuring up U.S. Infrastructure against Other Countries," PBS, February 18, 2018, https://www.pbs.org/newshour/nation/measuring-up-u-s-infrastructure-against-other-countries.

13 "Richard Nixon and Nikita Khrushchev Have a 'Kitchen Debate,'" History.com, November 13, 2009, https://www.history.com/this-day-in-history/nixon-and-khrushchev-have-a-kitchen-debate.

14 Glenn Chapman, "Kansas City, Kansas, Wins Google Broadband Nod," Phys.org, March 30, 2011, https://phys.org/news/2011-03-kansas-city-google-broadband.html.

15 Elise Ackerman, "How Kansas Won the Google Fiber Jackpot and Why California Never Will," *Forbes*, August 5, 2012, https://www.forbes.com/sites/eliseackerman/2012/08/04/how-kansas-won-the-google-fiber-jackpot-and-why-california-never-will/#5bffd2e14b76.

16 Rick Montgomery, "KC's Startup Village, a Google Fiber Inspiration, Is Gone. But It Wasn't a Failure," *The Kansas City Star*, January 14, 2019, https://www.kansascity.com/news/business/article223842985.html.

17 Kendra Chamberlain, "Municipal Broadband Is Roadblocked Or Outlawed In 25 States," Broadband Now, January 18, 2020, https://broadbandnow.com/report/municipal-broadband-roadblocks/.

18 Emily Badger, "How the Telecom Lobby Is Killing Municipal Broadband," CityLab, November 4, 2011, https://www.citylab.com/life/2011/11/telecom-lobby-killing-municipal-broadband/420/.

19 Alia E. Dastagir, "Trust No One? Americans Lack Faith in the Government, the Media and Each Other, Survey Finds," *USA Today*, July 23, 2019, https://www.usatoday.com/story/news/nation/2019/07/23/pew-study-american-trust-declines-government-media-and-each-other/1798963001/.

20 "Gautrain Rapid Rail Link," Global Infrastructure Hub, May 8, 2018, https://managingppp.gihub.org/case-studies/gautrain-rapid-rail-link/.

21 Tony Bovaird, "A Brief Intellectual History of the Public-Private Partnership Movement," *International Handbook on Public-Private Partnerships* (2010), Chapter 3, https://doi.org/10.4337/9781849804691.00010.

22 Ilan Dunsky, "The Success of P3 In Canada," Mondaq, August 8, 2013, http://www.mondaq.com/canada/x/256856/Government+Contracts+Procurement+PPP/The+Success+of+P3+in+Canada.

23 Patrick Sabol and Robert Puentes, "Private Capital, Public Good: Drivers of Successful Infrastructure Private-Public Partnerships," Brookings, July 2016, https://www.brookings.edu/wp-content/uploads/2016/07/BMPP_PrivateCapitalPublicGood.pdf.

24 "What Is the Rapid Bridge Replacement Project?" The Pennsylvania Rapid Bridge Replacement Project, http://parapidbridges.com/projectoverview.html.

25 "Public-Private Partnerships in the US: The State of the Market and the Road Ahead," PWC, November 2016, https://www.pwc.com/us/en/capital-projects-infrastructure/publications/assets/pwc-us-public-private-partnerships.pdf.

26 "What Is the Rapid Bridge Replacement Project?" The Pennsylvania Rapid Bridge Replacement Project, http://parapidbridges.com/projectoverview.html.

27 Ibid.

28 Dan McNichol, "The United States: The World's Largest Emerging P3 Market," AIG, https://www.aig.com/content/dam/aig/america-canada/us/documents/insights/final-p3-aig-whitepaper-brochure.pdf.

29 Ibid.

30 Morag Baird, "We Analyzed More Than 3,700 Public-Private Partnerships. Here's What We Found," *Brink*, December 6, 2018, https://www.brinknews.com/we-analyzed-over-3700-public-private-partnerships-heres-what-we-found/.

31 Ibid.

32 Bob Poole, "Removing Federal Barriers to P3 Infrastructure Investment," Jefferson Policy Journal, February 1, 2017, http://www.jeffersonpolicyjournal.com/removing-federal-barriers-to-p3-infrastructure-investment/.

33 "Federal Aid to State and Local Governments," Center on Budget and Policy Priorities, April 19, 2018, https://www.cbpp.org/research/state-budget-and-tax/federal-aid-to-state-and-local-governments?utm_source=feedburner.

34 "Public-Private Partnership (P3) Model State Legislation," BPC Action, December 17, 2015, https://bpcaction.org/2015/12/public-private-partnership-p3-model-state-legislation/.

35 Doug Shinkle and Gretchenn DuBois, "NCSL P3 State Legislative Update: 2016-2018," National Conference of State Legislatures, June 18, 2019, http://www.ncsl.org/research/transportation/ncsl-p3-update.aspx.

36 Ryan Holeywell, "Why Isn't the U.S. Better at Public-Private Partnerships?" Governing, February 2013, https://www.governing.com/topics/finance/gov-public-private-partnerships-in-america.html.

37 "Public Private Partnership Program," Texas Facilities Commission, June 2019, http://www.tfc.state.tx.us/divisions/facilities/prog/planning/p3/.

CHAPTER 4: A PORTABLE SOCIAL CONTRACT

1   Chris Isidore, "GM Made $22.6 Billion. Taxpayers Lost $10.6 Billion," CNNMoney, May 29, 2014, https://money.cnn.com/2014/05/29/news/companies/gm-profit-bailout/index.html.

2   "End of the Line for Four Generations at GM?" NBCNews.com, January 31, 2009, http://www.nbcnews.com/id/28951756/ns/business-autos/t/end-line-four-generations-gm/#.XsWs4sZ7kWp.

3   Yuki Noguchi, "Will Work for No Benefits: The Challenges of Being in the New Contract Workforce," NPR, January 23, 2018, https://www.npr.org/2018/01/23/579720874/will-work-for-no-benefits-the-challenges-of-being-in-the-new-contract-workforce.

4   Guy Berger, "Will This Year's College Grads Job-Hop More Than Previous Grads?" LinkedIn, April 12, 2016, https://blog.linkedin.com/2016/04/12/will-this-year_s-college-grads-job-hop-more-than-previous-grads.

5   Heather Long, "The New Normal: 4 Job Changes by the Time You're 32," CNNMoney, April 12, 2016, https://money.cnn.com/2016/04/12/news/economy/millennials-change-jobs-frequently/index.html.

6   Mitchell Hartman, "What Makes Gig Economy Workers Anxious?" Marketplace, March 8, 2018, https://www.marketplace.org/2018/03/08/gig-workers-and-economically-anxious-lifestyle/.

7   Jacob Passy, "Americans Are Plagued by Financial Anxiety—and It's Only Getting Worse," MarketWatch, May 8, 2018, https://www.marketwatch.com/story/americans-have-more-anxiety-about-paying-their-bills-than-they-did-a-year-ago-2018-05-08.

8   Monica Potts, "Americans Are More Vulnerable Than Ever, and the Gig
     Economy Isn't Helping," Talking Points Memo, October 29, 2018, https://
     talkingpointsmemo.com/feature/americans-are-more-vulnerable-than-ever-
     and-the-gig-economy-isnt-helping.

9   Marlene Y. Satter, "23 Percent of Full Time-Employees Lack
     Benefits," BenefitsPRO, January 22, 2018, https://www.benefitspro.
     com/2018/01/22/23-percent-of-full-time-employees-lack-benefits/?slret
     urn=20200420182530.

10   Jacob S. Hacker, "The Economy Is Strong. So Why Do So Many Americans
     Still Feel at Risk?" New York Times, May 21, 2019, https://www.nytimes.
     com/2019/05/21/opinion/trump-economy.html.

11   Katherine Newman, "Retirement Should Not Mean Hardship—but Many
     Older Americans Live in Poverty," Guardian, May 24, 2019, https://www.
     theguardian.com/us-news/2019/may/24/elder-poverty-america-hardship-
     retirement-economics.

12   Kathleen Elk, "How Much Money Americans Are Saving for Retirement—
     and How Much You Need If You Want to Retire by 65," CNBC, March 13,
     2019, https://www.cnbc.com/2019/03/12/most-americans-arent-saving-
     enough-to-retire-by-age-65.html.

13   "Why Millions of Americans Are Still Working Past the Age of 65," CBS
     News, December 12, 2018, https://www.cbsnews.com/news/retirement-age-
     changing-why-millions-of-americans-are-working-past-65/.

14   "Mortality in the United States: Past, Present, and Future," Penn Wharton
     Budget Model, June 27, 2016, https://budgetmodel.wharton.upenn.edu/
     issues/2016/1/25/mortality-in-the-united-states-past-present-and-future.

15   Melissa de Witte, "Americans Are Not Financially Prepared for Living
     Longer Lives, Stanford Study Finds," Stanford University, October 22, 2018,
     https://news.stanford.edu/press-releases/2018/10/22/americans-not-fi-age-
     study-finds/.

16   Bob Pisani, "Baby Boomers Face Retirement Crisis—Little Savings, High
     Health Costs and Unrealistic Expectations," CNBC, April 9, 2019, https://
     www.cnbc.com/2019/04/09/baby-boomers-face-retirement-crisis-little-
     savings-high-health-costs-and-unrealistic-expectations.html.

17   Andrew Van Dam, "Baby Boomers Are Retiring in Droves. Here Are
     Three Big Reasons for Concern," Chicago Tribune, March 1, 2019, https://
     www.chicagotribune.com/business/success/ct-biz-baby-boomers-retire-
     dollarsense-20190301-story.html.

18 Kathleen Elk, "Here's How Much the Average American Family Has Saved for Retirement," CNBC, August 1, 2017, https://www.cnbc. com/2016/09/12/heres-how-much-the-average-american-family-has-saved-for-retirement.html.

19 Mark J. Warshawsky and Andrew G. Biggs, "Income Inequality and Rising Health-Care Costs," *Wall Street Journal*, October 6, 2014, https://www.wsj. com/articles/mark-warshawsky-and-andrew-biggs-income-inequality-and-rising-health-care-costs-1412568847?wpisrc=nlwonkbk&.

20 Monique Morrissey, "The State of American Retirement: How 401(k)s Have Failed Most American Workers," Economic Policy Institute, https://www. epi.org/publication/retirement-in-america/#charts.

21 Kathleen Elk, "Here's How Much the Average American Family Has Saved for Retirement," CNBC, August 1, 2017, https://www.cnbc. com/2016/09/12/heres-how-much-the-average-american-family-has-saved-for-retirement.html.

22 Amy Whyte, "Most Companies Plan to Get Rid of Their Pension Liabilities," Institutional Investor, January 24, 2019, https://www.institutionalinvestor. com/article/b1cv15f120pxj3/Most-Companies-Plan-to-Get-Rid-of-Their-Pension-Liabilities.

23 Bob Pisani, "There's a Retirement Crisis in America Where Most Will Be Unable to Afford a 'Solid Life,'" CNBC, April 1, 2019, https://www.cnbc. com/2019/04/01/theres-a-retirement-crisis-in-america-where-most-will-be-unable-to-afford-a-solid-life.html.

24 Matthew Yglesias, "The Time Nancy Pelosi Saved Social Security," *Vox*, November 21, 2018, https://www.vox.com/policy-and-politics/2018/11/21/18103325/nancy-pelosi-social-security-privatization-bush-plan.

25 Alessandra Malito, "This Is Why You Shouldn't Count on Social Security," *MarketWatch*, July 7, 2018, https://www.marketwatch.com/story/this-is-why-you-shouldnt-count-on-social-security-2017-10-27.

26 "Monthly Statistical Snapshot, December 2019," Social Security Administration, January 2020, https://www.ssa.gov/policy/docs/quickfacts/stat_snapshot/.

27 Nick Wing, "17 Numbers That Will Make You Realize Just How Pathetic the Federal Minimum Wage Is," *HuffPost*, December 7, 2017, https://www. huffpost.com/entry/minimum-wage-increase-numbers_n_5868848.

28 Sean Williams, "Your Social Security Check Won't Cover Rent in These 8 States," *USA Today*, March 13, 2019, https://www.usatoday.com/story/money/personalfinance/retirement/2019/03/13/social-security-income-not-enough-cover-rent-check-8-states/39166629/.

29 Chris Farrell, "How Grim Is the Future of Retirement?" *MarketWatch*, August 7, 2019, https://www.marketwatch.com/story/how-grim-is-the-future-of-retirement-2019-08-06.

30 John Himics, interview by authors, phone, October 28, 2019.

31 Shaila Dewan, "How Obamacare Could Unlock Job Opportunities," *New York Times*, February 20, 2014, https://www.nytimes.com/2014/02/23/magazine/how-obamacare-could-unlock-job-opportunities.html.

32 Shayna Strom, "Protecting Workers in a Patchwork Economy," The Century Foundation, April 7, 2016, https://tcf.org/content/report/protecting-workers-patchwork-economy/?agreed=1&session=1.

33 Natalie Foster, Greg Nelson, and Libby Reder. "Portable Benefits Resource Guide," The Aspen Institute, 2016, https://assets.aspeninstitute.org/content/uploads/2016/07/resource_guide_final8-1.pdf?_.ga=2.36340128.1625205635.1568049696-863122461.1568049696.

34 Ibid.

35 "Preparing NYC's Economy and Workforce for the Next Wave of Automation," Center for an Urban Future: 4, https://nycfuture.org/pdf/Automation_Forum_Report.pdf.

36 "New State Ice Co. v. Liebmann," 285 US 262—Supreme Court (1932). https://scholar.google.com/scholar_case?case=14454584999299199739&q=New+State+Co.+v.+Liebmann,+285+U.S.+262+(1932)&hl=en&as_sdt=6,33&as_vis=1.

37 Nick Hanauer and David Rolf, "Portable Benefits for an Insecure Workforce," The American Prospect, February 23, 2017, https://prospect.org/article/portable-benefits-insecure-workforce.

38 "Saver Information," OregonSaves, https://saver.oregonsaves.com/.

39 Kristian Foden-Vencil, "State Rolls out OregonSaves Retirement Program," *The Seattle Times*, March 2, 2018, https://www.seattletimes.com/nation-world/state-rolls-out-oregonsaves-retirement-program/.

40 Tobias Read, interview by authors, email, February 19, 2020.

41 Ruth Reader, "Senator Mark Warner Has a New Plan to Protect Gig Economy Workers," *Fast Company*, February 26, 2019, https://www.fastcompany.com/90312184/senator-mark-warner-has-a-new-plan-to-protect-gig-economy-workers.

42 "Sen. Warner Announces Growing Support for Portable Benefits Legislation,"
    Mark R. Warner, June 20, 2018, https://www.warner.senate.gov/public/
    index.cfm/2018/6/sen-warner-announces-growing-support-for-portable-
    benefits-legislation.

43 "Google.org Funds Future of Work Initiative's Portable Benefits Efforts," The
    Aspen Institute, June 5, 2018, https://www.aspeninstitute.org/blog-posts/
    google-org-future-of-work-initiative-grant-2018/.

44 Suzi Levine, "Providing 21st Century Benefits: A Snapshot from Washington
    State's New Paid Family and Medical Program," The Aspen Institute, May
    7, 2019, https://www.aspeninstitute.org/blog-posts/providing-21st-century-
    benefits-a-snapshot-from-washington-state/.

CHAPTER 5: EVERYDAY ENTREPRENEURS

1   Justin McCarthy, "U.S. Confidence in Organized Religion Remains Low,"
    Gallup, October 7, 2019, https://news.gallup.com/poll/259964/confidence-
    organized-religion-remains-low.aspx.

2   Victor Hwang, "Want Job Creation and a Thriving Middle Class? Support
    Your Local Entrepreneurs," *The Hill*, June 3, 2019, https://thehill.com/
    opinion/finance/439190-want-job-creation-and-a-thriving-middle-class-
    support-your-local.

3   Victor Hwang, "Breaking Down Barriers to Capital Access," Ewing Marion
    Kauffman Foundation, May 23, 2019, https://www.kauffman.org/currents/
    breaking-down-barriers-to-capital-access/.

4   Charles Euchner, "Scale Up New York: Creating Middle Class Jobs by
    Growing New York City's Small Business," Center for an Urban Future: 13,
    November 2016, https://nycfuture.org/pdf/CUF_Scale_Up_New_York.pdf.

5   Victor Hwang, Sameeksha Desai, and Ross Baird, "Access to Capital for
    Entrepreneurs: Removing Barriers," Ewing Marion Kauffman Foundation,
    March 2019, https://www.kauffman.org/-/media/kauffman_org/
    entrepreneurship-landing-page/capital-access/capitalreport_042519.pdf.

6   Jamie Johnson, "3 Key Facts About Small Business Lending," US Chamber
    of Commerce, May 22, 2019, https://www.uschamber.com/co/run/finance/
    small-business-lending-facts.

7   Justin Song, "Average Small Business Loan Interest Rates in 2020: Comparing
    Top Lenders," ValuePenguin, January 21, 2020, https://www.valuepenguin.
    com/average-small-business-loan-interest-rates.

8   "The Opportunity Bank: A Trillion Dollars in New Small Business Lending,"
    Third Way, February 15, 2019, https://www.thirdway.org/report/the-
    opportunity-bank-a-trillion-dollars-in-new-small-business-lending.

9   Ibid.

10 Shuyi Shang, "Why Is It So Hard to Get a Small Business Loan?" Bento for
    Business, March 15, 2016, https://bentoforbusiness.com/why-is-it-so-hard-
    to-get-a-small-business-loan.

11 "The Opportunity Bank: A Trillion Dollars in New Small Business Lending,"
    Third Way, February 15, 2019, https://www.thirdway.org/report/the-
    opportunity-bank-a-trillion-dollars-in-new-small-business-lending.

12 Charles Euchner, "Scale Up New York: Creating Middle Class Jobs by
    Growing New York City's Small Business," Center for an Urban Future: 12,
    November 2016, https://nycfuture.org/pdf/CUF_Scale_Up_New_York.pdf.

13 "Business Loan Interest Rates: How to Get Low Rates," Fundera, https://
    www.fundera.com/business-loans/guides/business-loan-interest-rate.

14 "The Opportunity Bank: A Trillion Dollars in New Small Business Lending,"
    Third Way, February 15, 2019, https://www.thirdway.org/report/the-
    opportunity-bank-a-trillion-dollars-in-new-small-business-lending.

15 Benjamin Spillman, "Delivering a New Downtown," *The Las Vegas Review
    Journal*, http://www.melissahyang.com/lvrj/.

16 Natalie Bruzda, "Woman Opens 3rd Las Vegas Eatery after Overcoming
    Addiction," *The Las Vegas Review Journal*, February 15, 2018, https://www.
    reviewjournal.com/local/summerlin/woman-opens-3rd-las-vegas-eatery-
    after-overcoming-addiction/.

17 Pat Mertz Esswein, "Small-Business Success Story: Bryson City Bicycles,"
    Kiplinger's Personal Finance, June 7, 2018, https://www.kiplinger.com/
    article/business/T049-C000-S002-small-business-success-story-bryson-
    city-bicycles.html.

18 Victor Hwang, Sameeksha Desai, and Ross Baird, "Access to Capital for
    Entrepreneurs: Removing Barriers," Ewing Marion Kauffman Foundation,
    March 2019, https://www.kauffman.org/-/media/kauffman_org/
    entrepreneurship-landing-page/capital-access/capitalreport_042519.pdf.

19 Tanya Prive, "What Returns Can I Expect from Startup Investing," *Forbes*,
    April 28, 2016, https://www.forbes.com/sites/tanyaprive/2016/04/28/what-
    returns-can-i-expect-from-startup-investing/#197c15c67964.

20 "Welcome to Village Capital," Village Capital, https://vilcap.com/.

21 Karen Mills, "Why Small-Business Lending Has Not Recovered," *Forbes*, August 4, 2014, https://www.forbes.com/sites/ hbsworkingknowledge/2014/08/04/why-small-business-lending-has-not-recovered/#2a8d2ac05587.

22 Rohit Arora, "Small Business Loan Approvals at Banks Hit Record Highs," *Forbes*, August 7, 2019, https://www.forbes.com/sites/ rohitarora/2019/08/07/small-business-loan-approvals-at-banks-hit-record-highs/#128e19507563.

23 Jim Nussle, "Small Businesses and Credit Unions: For the Good of America," *HuffPost*, April 30, 2017, https://www.huffpost.com/entry/small-businesses-and-cred_b_9810786?guccounter=1.

24 Craig R. Everett, "2018 Q4 Private Capital Access Index Report," Pepperdine University, October 25, 2018, https://digitalcommons.pepperdine.edu/cgi/ viewcontent.cgi?article=1016&context=gsbm_pcm_pca.

25 "Why Banks Don't Lend to Small Businesses," West Philadelphia Financial Services Institution, November 14, 2019, https://wpfsi.com/banks-dont-lend-small-businesses/.

26 Spencer M. Cowan, "Patterns of Disparity: Small Business Lending in the Chicago and Los Angeles-San Diego Regions," Woodstock Institute, January 2017, http://www.documentcloud.org/documents/5028189-Chicago-and-LASD-Report-CC-License-Update.html.

27 Ruth Simon and Coulter Jones, "Goodbye, George Bailey: Decline of Rural Lending Crimps Small-Town Business," *Wall Street Journal*, December 25, 2017, https://www.wsj.com/articles/goodbye-george-bailey-decline-of-rural-lending-crimps-small-town-business-1514219515.

28 Spencer M. Cowan, "Patterns of Disparity: Small Business Lending in the Chicago and Los Angeles-San Diego Regions," Woodstock Institute, January 2017, http://www.documentcloud.org/documents/5028189-Chicago-and-LASD-Report-CC-License-Update.html.

29 "Firmament Group Study Reveals Small Business Owners Struggle to Access Needed Capital for Expansion and Growth," *Business Insider*, July 26, 2018, https://markets.businessinsider.com/news/stocks/firmament-group-study-reveals-small-business-owners-struggle-to-access-needed-capital-for-expansion-and-growth-1027403987.

30 "Small Businesses in America: Costly Credit and Growth Challenges," *Wall Street Journal*, March 6, 2018, https://youtu.be/om06jmPJiqU.

31 Gary Stockton, "Women Business Owners Face Challenges Getting Capital," Experian, March 27, 2018, http://www.experian.com/blogs/small-business-matters/2018/03/27/women-business-owners-getting-capital/.

32 Ruth Simon and Tom McGinty, "Loan Rebound Misses Black Businesses," *Wall Street Journal*, March 15, 2014, https://www.wsj.com/articles/no-headline-available-1394831256.

33 "Examining the Unique Opportunities and Challenges Facing Rural Small Businesses," Small Business Majority, February 12, 2019, https://smallbusinessmajority.org/our-research/entrepreneurship-freelance-economy/examining-unique-opportunities-and-challenges-facing-rural-small-businesses.

34 Ruth Simon and Coulter Jones, "Goodbye, George Bailey: Decline of Rural Lending Crimps Small-Town Business," *Wall Street Journal*, December 25, 2017, https://www.wsj.com/articles/goodbye-george-bailey-decline-of-rural-lending-crimps-small-town-business-1514219515.

35 "Why Banks Don't Lend to Small Businesses," West Philadelphia Financial Services Institution, November 14, 2019, https://wpfsi.com/banks-dont-lend-small-businesses/.

36 Victor Hwang, Sameeksha Desai, and Ross Baird, "Access to Capital for Entrepreneurs: Removing Barriers," Ewing Marion Kauffman Foundation, March 2019, https://www.kauffman.org/-/media/kauffman_org/entrepreneurship-landing-page/capital-access/capitalreport_042519.pdf.

37 Karen Mills, "Why Small-Business Lending Has Not Recovered," *Forbes*, August 4, 2014, https://www.forbes.com/sites/hbsworkingknowledge/2014/08/04/why-small-business-lending-has-not-recovered/#651056805587.

38 Charles Euchner, "Scale Up New York: Creating Middle Class Jobs by Growing New York City's Small Business," Center for an Urban Future: 14, November 2016, https://nycfuture.org/pdf/CUF_Scale_Up_New_York.pdf.

39 Spencer M. Cowan, "Patterns of Disparity: Small Business Lending in the Chicago and Los Angeles-San Diego Regions," Woodstock Institute, January 2017, http://www.documentcloud.org/documents/5028189-Chicago-and-LASD-Report-CC-License-Update.html.

40 "Small Business Administration 7(a) Loan Guaranty Program," Congressional Research Service, October 15, 2019, https://fas.org/sgp/crs/misc/R41146.pdf.

41 "The Agenda for America's Entrepreneurs: Access to Capital," Small Business Majority, https://smallbusinessmajority.org/sites/default/files/agenda/2019-Access-to-Capital-Policy-Agenda-2-pager_0.pdf.

42 Matt Tatham, "Student Loan Debt Climbs to $1.4 Trillion in 2019," Experian, July 24, 2019, https://www.experian.com/blogs/ask-experian/state-of-student-loan-debt/.

43 Ibid.

44 "The Opportunity Bank: A Trillion Dollars in New Small Business Lending," Third Way, February 15, 2019, https://www.thirdway.org/report/the-opportunity-bank-a-trillion-dollars-in-new-small-business-lending.

45 "Community Advantage: A Pilot Loan Program," Small Business Administration, https://www.sba.gov/sites/default/files/resource_files/Community_Advantage_Flyer_with_Lenders.pdf.

46 "The Agenda for America's Entrepreneurs: Access to Capital," Small Business Majority, https://smallbusinessmajority.org/sites/default/files/agenda/2019-Access-to-Capital-Policy-Agenda-2-pager_0.pdf.

47 "Washington Office Center," Small Business Administration, https://www.sba.gov/offices/headquarters/osbdc.

48 "What We Do," Minority Business Development Agency, December 18, 2018, https://www.mbda.gov/about/whatwedo.

49 "SBA Increases Opportunities for Women Entrepreneurs with Opening of New Women's Business Centers," PR Newswire, June 27, 2018, https://www.prnewswire.com/news-releases/sba-increases-opportunities-for-women-entrepreneurs-with-opening-of-new-womens-business-centers-300625323.html.

50 "Rural Microentrepreneur Assistance Program," US Department of Agriculture, https://www.rd.usda.gov/sites/default/files/fact-sheet/508_RD_FS_RBS_RMAP.pdf.

51 "Rural Business Development Grants (RBDG)," US Department of Agriculture, https://www.rd.usda.gov/files/fact-sheet/RD-Fact-Sheet-RBS-RBDG.pdf.

52 "Rural Development," US Department of Agriculture, https://www.rd.usda.gov/programs-services/intermediary-relending-program.

53 "Policy Agenda: Access to Capital," Small Business Majority, July 3, 2019, https://smallbusinessmajority.org/policy-agenda/access-capital.

54 Rohit Arora, "Raising the Credit Union Lending Cap Would Benefit Small Businesses," *Forbes*, January 26, 2017, https://www.forbes.com/sites/rohitarora/2017/01/25/raising-the-credit-union-lending-cap-would-benefit-small-businesses/#1b67d44e1328.

55 "The Agenda for America's Entrepreneurs: Access to Capital," Small Business Majority, https://smallbusinessmajority.org/sites/default/files/agenda/2019-Access-to-Capital-Policy-Agenda-2-pager_0.pdf.

56 Victor Hwang, Sameeksha Desai, and Ross Baird, "Access to Capital for Entrepreneurs: Removing Barriers," Ewing Marion Kauffman Foundation, March 2019, https://www.kauffman.org/-/media/kauffman_org/entrepreneurship-landing-page/capital-access/capitalreport_042519.pdf.

57 "Microloans," AltCap, https://www.alt-cap.org/microloans.

58 Victor Hwang, Sameeksha Desai, and Ross Baird, "Access to Capital for Entrepreneurs: Removing Barriers," Ewing Marion Kauffman Foundation, March 2019, https://www.kauffman.org/-/media/kauffman_org/entrepreneurship-landing-page/capital-access/capitalreport_042519.pdf.

CONCLUSION: BEYOND THE REBOUND

1 Tara Golshan, "Abigail Spanberger Elected to US House of Representatives: A Democrat Just Ousted a Tea Party Star," *Vox*, November 7, 2018, https://www.vox.com/2018/11/6/18070272/house-midterm-results-virginia-seventh-abigail-spanberger-winner.

2 Patrick Wilson, "Fueled by Suburban Votes, Spanberger Beats Brat in 7th District House Race," *Richmond Times-Dispatch*, November 7, 2018, https://www.richmond.com/news/local/government-politics/fueled-by-suburban-votes-spanberger-beats-brat-in-7th-district-house-race/article_e757b2af-7329-55cb-992e-c6fcdb3c62d1.html.

3 Andy Beshear and John Bel Edwards, "How Democrats Can Win, Everywhere," *Washington Post*, November 25, 2019, https://www.washingtonpost.com/opinions/2019/11/25/how-democrats-can-beat-trump-everywhere/.

4 Gary Younge, "The Democrats Must Do More Than Simply Oppose Donald Trump," *Guardian*, August 9, 2018, https://www.theguardian.com/commentisfree/2018/aug/09/democrats-oppose-trump-republicans-passive.

5   Reid J. Epstein and Sydney Ember, "Bernie Sanders Calls His Brand
    of Socialism a Pathway to Beating Trump," *New York Times*, June 12,
    2019, https://www.nytimes.com/2019/06/12/us/politics/bernie-sanders-
    socialism.html.

6   Ed Kilgore, "Republicans Going All-Out Red Scare in Off-Year Elections,"
    NYMag, October 31, 2019, http://nymag.com/intelligencer/2019/10/
    republican-electoral-strategy-brand-democrats-as-socialist.html.

7   Nate Cohn and Kevin Quealy, "The Democratic Electorate on Twitter Is Not
    the Actual Democratic Electorate," *New York Times*, April 9, 2019, https://
    www.nytimes.com/interactive/2019/04/08/upshot/democratic-electorate-
    twitter-real-life.html.

8   David Leonhardt, "Democrats, Stop Helping Trump," *New York Times*,
    September 8, 2019, https://www.nytimes.com/2019/09/08/opinion/
    democrats-2020-trump.html.

9   Deborah Santostefano, "Youth Service Corps," Hartford.Gov—Youth Service
    Corps, http://www.hartford.gov/collaborations/2443-ysc.

10 Kira Lerner, "How One Conservative Group Plans to Maintain Republicans'
    Grip on State Legislatures," Talking Points Memo, October 21, 2019,
    https://talkingpointsmemo.com/feature/alec-gerrymandering-courts.

11 Jonathan Martin and Denise Lu, "Democrats' Best Recruitment Tool?
    President Trump," *New York Times*, April 6, 2018, https://www.nytimes.
    com/interactive/2018/04/06/us/surge-in-democratic-candidates-for-the-
    house.html.

12 Alex Seitz-Wald, "Thousands of Would-Be Democratic Candidates Flood
    States in Trump Backlash," NBCNews.com, March 22, 2017, https://
    www.nbcnews.com/storyline/democrats-vs-trump/thousands-would-be-
    democrat-candidates-flood-states-trump-backlash-n736761.

INDEX

"A Nation at Risk," 47
Affordable Care Act of 2010, 115, 154
Aid to Families with Dependent
    Children (AFDC), 25
AltCap, 151
American Dream, xvii, 4, 9, 13, 15, 26,
    47, 50, 103, 125, 127, 135
American Legislative Exchange Council
    (ALEC), 161
American Road and Transportation
    Building Association, 79
American Society of Civil Engineers, 80
AmeriCorps program, 160
Anderson, Bria, 36–37
Arora, Rohit, 149

Baby College. *See* Harlem Children's
    Zone Baby College
Baker, Danielle, 131, 139–140
Barton, Todd, 19
Berger, Guy, 104

Beshear, Andy, 155, 156
Biz2Credit, 149
Black Car Fund, 117
Bloomberg, Michael, 34, 35
Brandeis, Justice Louis, 119
Brat, Dave, 153–155
Bryson City Bicycles case, 135
Bussanmas, Sister Corita, 41

Camden City School District case,
    57–58, 60
Campos, Sylvia, 75–76
Canada, Geoffrey, 29, 47
Cantor, Eric, 153
Center for an Urban Future (CUF), 118,
    129, 132, 145
Childcare issues
    access to, 18–25, 36–38, 41–43, 44
    affordability of care and, 36–37
    childcare, economic return on
        investment in, 39–41

childcare, social return on investment
in, 41–43
childcare-related absenteeism, cost
of, 39
COVID-19 pandemic and, xiv–xv
deficient/unregulated childcare
options and, 23–24, 38
disadvantaged families and, 41–43
early childhood education initiatives
and, 26–28, 30, 34, 38, 41–43
early childhood language
development initiatives and,
34–36
economic/productivity disruption
and, 18–25, 36–37, 39, 40–41
expanded services, government
support of, 37–38
government support, absence of, 23,
24–25, 27–28
home visitation programs and, 30
Houlahan maternity leave case and,
20–22
infant care initiatives and, 28–31,
36–38
informal childcare networks and,
23–24
opportunity agenda and, xv
paid family leave policy and, 31–33
parenting education initiatives and,
28–31
school success and, 42–43
screen time, excess of, 24, 26
women in the workforce, absence of,
20–25, 39–41
"workplace ghosts" and, 23–25
See also Education reform;
Opportunity Agenda;
Working-/middle-class issues
Children's Health Insurance Program
(CHIP), 23
Clinton, William J., 149, 160

Clinton, Hillary R., 17, 122
Coalition for Queens. See Pursuit
nonprofit organization
Community Advantage Pilot Program,
148
Community Development Financial
Institutions (CDFIs), 149–150
COVID-19 pandemic, xi, 18, 50
change, opportunity for, xiii–xiv, xvii
childcare systems and, xiv–xv
economic crisis and, xi–xii
economic weaknesses, exposure/
acceleration of, xii, xvi, 5, 78
education reform and, xv
employer-supplied benefits,
disappearance of, xvi, 123
"for you" policy agenda and, xii–xiv,
xvii
infrastructure projects and, xv
leadership effectiveness, need for, xii,
xiii–xiv
local political leaders, role of, xiii
public-private partnerships, role
of, xv
recovery effort and, xii, xiii–xiv, 123
small business capital, access to, xii,
xvi, 139
unemployment and, xvi
workers' benefits and, xvi, 123
Crawfordsville case, 17–19
Cutler, Diane, 135

de Blasio, Bill, 38
Democratic renaissance, 1, 4
electorate, disillusionment of, 2, 4
governing majority, resumption of, 2
policy stagnation and, 2–3
Republican agenda, opposition to, 2
Republican implosion and, 3–4

sustainable agenda/narrative of, 2,
3–4, 12–13
2016 presidential election and, 2
2018 midterm election and, 1–2
See also New Democratic agenda;
Opportunity Agenda; Rebound
politics; Republican agenda
Dixon, Byron, 58
Donofree, Dana, 142–143
"Downtown Project" campaign, 134
Dropbox, 129

Early childhood education initiatives,
26–28, 30, 34, 38, 39, 41–43, 44
Economic policy
childcare, access to, 18–25, 36–37,
39, 40–41
childcare, economic return on
investment in, 39–41
childcare, social return on investment
in, 41–43
consumer spending, economic
growth and, 8
COVID-19 pandemic and, xi–xiv
Crawfordsville case example and,
17–19
downward mobility, fear of, 5
early childhood education policy
and, 26–28
economic dynamism, examples of, 78
economic justice goals and, 85–86
economic weaknesses, exposure/
acceleration of, xii, xiii
education reform and, 46, 47, 48–49,
50
"for you" policy agenda and, xii–xiv,
11–13, 18–20
gig economy, portable social contract
and, 100–103
global market growth and, xi–xii

immigration, politics of 13–14
income inequality, impact of, 125
industrial heartland, manufacturing
downturn and, 13
inequity issue and, xii, 7
infrastructure projects and, 76–78, 80
job market conditions and, 4–5, 46,
47, 48–49
maternity leave policy and, 20–22
minimum wage policy and, 3, 8
middle class, survival of, xii, xiv
paid family leave policy and, 31–33
small business capital, access to, xii,
xvi
technology/globalization, worker
vulnerability and, 4–5
trickle-down economics and, 122
"We're losing," Trump's core message
of, 78–81
women in the workforce and, 20–25,
39–41
workforce skill development
initiatives and, 5
workforce skills, deficiencies in, 5
"workplace ghosts" and, 23–25
See also Entrepreneur Agenda;
Entrepreneurial enterprise;
Opportunity Agenda; Social
contract portability
Economic Policy Institute, 108
Education reform, 45
automation/technology systems,
demands of, 50–51
Camden City School District case
example and, 57–58, 60
charter school companies, significant
investments from, 57–58
cost of, 68
COVID-19 pandemic and, xv
digital divide and, xv

disadvantaged/marginalized
communities and, 66
distance learning and, xv
dropout rates and, 42–43, 58
early childhood education,
importance of, 26–28, 30, 34, 38,
39, 41–43, 44
early childhood language
development initiatives and,
34–36
economic conditions, alignment
with, 46, 47, 48, 50, 52, 61–64,
69–72
emerging fields, employment in, 69
existing education institutions,
improvement of, 65–68
"for you" policy agenda and, 48–49,
50–54, 59–60, 62–64
GI Bill, impact of, 46
globalization pressures and, 48,
61–64
graduation rates and, 58, 63
immersive learning opportunities
and, 60–64
Industrial Age, demands of, 45–46,
48, 51–54, 61–64
K-5 Plus program and, 67–68
lifelong learning, new commitment
to, 69–72
macro perspective on, 51–52
micro perspective on, 52–53
obsolete systems, reluctant
replacement of, 58–59, 61
one-room schoolhouses, replacement
of, 46
Operation Breakthrough and, 41–43
opportunity agenda and, xv
opportunity-centered policy agenda
and, 48–49, 59–60, 62–64,
66–67, 69–72

P-TECH program/immersive
learning and, 61–63, 64
parent involvement in, 49
Providence Public School District
case example and, 59
public education, declining
confidence in, 48–49
public-private partnerships and,
71–72
Pursuit nonprofit organization, skill
development and, 69–71
Ranken Technical College case
example and, 63–64
remedial education, mediocre
educational experience and,
47–48
return on investment data and,
66–67
school building-based toxins and, 79
school day/year, extension of, 65–68
skills gap, remediation of, xv
teacher compensation/job duties and,
55–57
teacher unions/tenure, vilification
of, 57, 58
twenty-first century needs and,
46–47, 48, 50, 51–54, 60, 61–64,
69–72
universal capacities, development of,
51–52, 61
work skills gap, closing of, 49, 50–54,
61–64, 66, 69–72
See also Childcare issues;
Opportunity Agenda
Edwards, John Bel, 155, 156
Electorate
alienation of, 1, 2, 7–8
American systems, unresponsiveness
of, 6, 7
brain-dead government, frustration
with, 14

faith in government, loss of, 10, 14
"for you" policy agenda and, 7–8,
    12–13
immigration issue and, 13–14
infrastructure projects, need for,
    75–78, 79
Medicare for All promise and, 7–8,
    10–11
political loyalties and, xi
racism/xenophobia and, 14, 78
real-world problems, solutions to,
    6–9, 10, 11, 13
undecided voters and, xi
unwinnable voters and, xi
working-/middle-class perspectives
    and, 6–8, 9, 10–11
See also Childcare issues; Democratic
    renaissance; Economic policy;
    Education reform; "For you"
    policy agenda; New Democratic
    agenda; Rebound politics;
    Republican agenda; Working-/
    middle-class issues
EMILY's List, 163
Entrepreneur Agenda, 146
AltCap microlender and, 151
capital, equitable access to, 146, 150
Community Advantage Pilot
    Program, permanent
    authorization for, 148
Community Development Financial
    Institutions, increased funding
    for, 149–150
credit union funding streams,
    tapping into, 149
Department of Agriculture programs
    and, 149
federal government loan guarantees,
    expansion of, 147
"for you" policy agenda and, 146–152
Great Recession, lessons from, 148

growth mindset, encouragement
    of, 148
lender competition, increase in, 149
loan approval requirements, reform
    of, 147–148
microfinancing and, 151
middle-out economic growth,
    resources for, 146
minority/women entrepreneurs,
    support of, 148–149
New Market Tax Credit program
    and, 150
The Object Enthusiast case example
    and, 150–151
Opportunity Zones and, 150
opportunity-centered political
    agenda and, 146–152
partnership formation, access to
    capital and, 150
private/philanthropic/nonprofit
    sectors, role of, 150, 151
rural entrepreneurs, support of,
    148–149
Small Business Administration,
    reorientation of, 146–150
small business financial regulations,
    review of, 148, 149
small business loans, pooling of, 150
student loan debt, barrier of, 147
underserved markets, permanent
    targeting of, 148
See also Entrepreneurial enterprise;
    Opportunity Agenda
Entrepreneurial enterprise, 125
Baker, Danielle, case example of, 131,
    139–140, 144
banks/financial institutions, role
    of, 130–133, 135, 136–137,
    138–140, 141–145
big businesses, advantaged financing
    of, 131–132, 139

Bryson City Bicycles case example
and, 135
capital, expanded access to, 128,
129–133, 134, 135–137
capital financing, curtailed flow of,
137–144
community/regional banks, rural
small business support and,
139–140, 144–145
credit deserts and, 139–140, 144
disadvantaged borrowers, capital
access for, 141–146
Donofree, Dana, case example of,
142–143
"Downtown Project" campaign and,
134
entrepreneurial ecosystem,
development of, xvi–xvii
everyday entrepreneurs, support of,
126–128, 133, 134, 135–137
Fin Gourmet restaurant case
example and, 136–137
"for you" policy agenda and, 128,
133, 142, 143
government support, dynamic
partnership role and, 127–128
Great Recession, impact of, 131–132,
139, 145
interest rates, burden of, 132
microfinance organizations and, 132
millennial generation entrepreneurs
and, 141–142, 144
minority entrepreneurs and, 143, 144
opportunity agenda and, xvi–xvii
opportunity-centered policy agenda
and, 126–128, 130–131, 135,
140, 141, 145–146, 150–152
optimism, innovation engine of, 125
portable benefits principle and, xvi
Ross, Shelton, case example of,
135–136

second-bottom-line motivation and,
136
small business failures and, 132–133
small businesses, economic growth
and, 126–127, 133, 138
start-up funding, elusive nature of,
130–132
tech bubble, success within, 125–126,
129, 137
venture capitalists, role of, 129–130,
134, 136, 137
Village Capital, social impact-
oriented financing and, 136–137
women entrepreneurs and, 142–143,
144
Young, Natalie, case example of,
133–135
See also Economic policy;
Entrepreneur Agenda;
Globalization pressures;
Opportunity Agenda
EyeVerify company, 84

Facebook, 129
Family and Medical Leave Act of 1993,
31–32
Family leave policy, 3, 31–33
Family values agenda, 31, 44
Federal Highway Administration
(FHWA), 79
FedEx Institute of Technology, 72
Fin Gourmet restaurant case, 136–137
First Ascent Design case, 110–113
Flores, Rene, 102
"For you" policy agenda
childcare, access to, xiv–xv, 18–25,
36–38, 40–41, 43–44
childcare, economic return on
investment in, 39–41

childcare, social return on investment in, 41–43
COVID-19 pandemic, response to, xii–xiv, xvii
Crawfordsville case example and, 18–20
early childhood education policy and, 26–28, 34, 38, 39, 41–43, 44
early childhood language development initiatives and, 24–26
education reform programs and, xv, 48–49, 50–54, 59–60, 62–64
entrepreneurial enterprise, government support of, xvi–xvii, 127–128, 133, 142, 146–152
improved lives/reduced costs and, 11
infant care initiatives and, 28–31
infrastructure projects and, xv, 76–78, 82–86, 91
internet access projects and, 82–86
maternity leave policy and, 20–22
Medicare for All and, 9–10
opportunity-centered policy agenda and, 11–13, 15
paid family leave policy and, 31–33
parenting education initiatives and, 28–31
policy/governing agendas and, 7–9, 11
Portable Social Contract framework and, 118–124
progressive agenda, defection from, 122–123
public-private partnerships, role of, 12, 71–72, 83–85
rebound political strategies and, 160–163
skills gap, closing of, 49, 50–54

See also Childcare issues; Education reform; Entrepreneurial enterprise; Infrastructure projects; New Democratic agenda; Opportunity Agenda; Portable Social Contract framework; Rebound politics; Social contract portability
Foxx, Anthony R., 11, 12
Future policies. *See* Opportunity Agenda; Rebound politics

Garner, Jennifer, 29
General Motors (GM), 99–100
GI Bill of 1944, 46
Gig economy, xvi, 100–103, 104, 105, 114, 118–122, 123
Globalization pressures
  American job market conditions and, 4–5, 123–124
  entrepreneurial ecosystem and, 126
  infrastructure improvements and, 80–81
  mediocre American education and, 47–48
Google, 82–85, 121
Great Depression, 109
Great Recession, 100–101, 131–132, 139, 145, 148
Great Society policies, 7, 38
Green New Deal policies, 146
Green, Rollin, 99–100, 102, 104, 113, 123
Grisham, Michelle Lujan, 67, 68
Griswold, Natasha, 128

Hacker, Jacob, 105
Harlem Children's Zone Baby College, 29, 30

Head Start program, 29, 38
Health care policy, 3
    health care coverage portability and,
        115
    Healthy Families America program
        and, 30
    paid family leave policy and, 31–33
    paid medical leave programs and,
        121–122
    rising health care costs, 107,
        112–113
    See also Medicare for All
Healthy Families America program, 30
Hidden Tribes project, 159
Himics, John, 110–113, 124
Himics, Pauline, 110–113, 124
Holland, Julie, 32
Houlahan, Chrissy, 20–22
Hsieh, Tony, 134
Hsu, Jukay, 69–70, 71

Immigration policy, 13–14, 154
Individual Security Accounts (ISAs),
    118–119, 120, 121
Industrial Age, 45–46, 48, 51–54, 61–64,
    114
Infrastructure projects, 75–76
    bid-and-build system and, 93–94
    bonded out projects and, 94–95
    bureaucratic incompetence,
        reminders of, 76–77, 79, 94, 96
    business expansion/economic growth
        and, 84, 85, 89–90
    Chinese infrastructure investments
        and, 80
    competing national economies,
        prosperity of, 80–81, 92
    decaying infrastructure, cost of,
        79–80
    federal deficit spending, liability
        of, 77
    internet access and, 79, 82–86
    job creation and, 89–90
    municipal analytics capability,
        strengthening of, 84
    New Deal programs and, 93
    One Gigabit to the Home project
        and, 82–85
    opportunity agenda and, xv
    opportunity-centered policy agenda
        and, 76–78, 81, 85–86, 89–90, 91
    Pennsylvania Rapid Bridge
        Replacement Program and,
        90–91
    Port of Baltimore project and, 88–89
    public-private partnerships, role of,
        xv, 83–91, 92, 93–97
    return on investment in, 93, 94–95
    structurally deficient bridges and,
        79, 90–91
    tax-and-spend regime, distancing
        from, 77
    telecommunications network
        improvements and, 83–85
    underinvestment in, 92–93
    United States' standing relative to,
        80–81
    "We're losing," Trump's core message
        of, 78–81
    world-class infrastructure, desire for,
        77–78
    See also "For you" policy agenda;
        Opportunity Agenda
Intermediary Relending Program, 149
Internet access, 79, 82–86
Ivy, Antonio, 104–105

James, Sly, 12, 32, 47, 83
James, William, 46

Job lock paralysis, 111–113, 114
Job market. *See* Economic policy;
    Education reform; Working-/
    middle-class issues
Johnson, Lyndon B., 7, 38
Johnson, Marietta, 46
J.P. Morgan, 72

K-5 Plus program, 67–68
Kauffman Foundation, 136
Kennedy, John F., 160
Khrushchev, Nikita, 81

Leonhardt, David, 159
Lesbian/gay/bisexual/transgender
    (LGBT) rights, 154
LevelUp program, 70–71
Linke, Rebecca, 39–40
LinkedIn, 104
Luu, Lula, 136–137
Lyft, 115, 116, 117

Majors, Martin, 106
Majors, Vivian, 106
Maternity leave policy, 20–22
Media reporting, 9
Medicare for All policy, 3
    compelling idea of, 10
    electorate perspectives on, 7–8,
        10–11
    ideal goals of, 11
Middle class. *See* Working-/middle-class
    issues
Miller, Stephen, 78
Minimum wage policy, 3, 8
Minority Business Development Agency,
    148

New Deal policies, 93
New Democratic agenda, 3–4
    big government gospel and, 4, 5,
        7, 10
    bureaucratic bloat/bungling and,
        5–6, 7
    coalition, building of, 4
    COVID-19 pandemic, response to,
        xii–xiv, xvii
    defensive campaigns/governance
        and, 7
    disruption, readiness for, 4
    economic policy and, 4–5, 8
    "for you" policy agenda and, xii–xiv,
        xvii, 7–8, 9, 10–11, 15
    free enterprise, belief in, 151–152
    greater good, aspirational goal of, 4
    idea generation, winning strategy
        of, 9
    Medicare for All, electorate
        perceptions of, 7–8, 10–11
    messaging failure and, 5, 8, 9
    moderate Republicans, appeal to, xii
    national constituency, needs of, 8–9
    opportunity, focus on, 4, 6, 9
    real-world problems, solutions to,
        6–9, 11
    workforce skill development
        initiatives and, 5
    working-/middle-class, opportunity
        for, xiv, xvi
    working-/middle-class perspectives
        and, 6–8, 9, 10–11
    See also Democratic renaissance;
        Entrepreneur Agenda;
        Opportunity Agenda; Policy
        stagnation; Portable Social
        Contract framework; Rebound
        politics
New Market Tax Credit program, 150
Nissan factory case, 104–105

Nixon, Richard M., 43, 81
Nurse-Family Partnership program, 30

Obama, Barack H., xii, 7, 11, 18, 115,
    162
The Object Enthusiast case, 150–151
One Gigabit to the Home project, 82–85
Operation Breakthrough, 41–42
Opportunity Agenda, xiv, 2–3, 11
    childcare, access to, xiv–xv,
        18–25, 28, 36–38, 40–41, 43–44
    childcare challenge, government
        response to, 23–25, 27–28,
        37–38
    childcare services, expansion of,
        37–38, 43–44
    childcare services, social return on
        investment in, 41–43
    childcare subsidies, economic return
        on investment in, 39–41
    COVID-19 pandemic, impact of,
        xii–xiv
    Crawfordsville case example and,
        17–19
    early childhood education initiatives
        and, 26–28, 30, 34, 38, 39,
        41–43, 44
    early childhood language
        development initiatives and,
        34–36
    education reform initiatives and, xv,
        48–49, 50–54, 59–60, 62–64,
        66–67, 69–72
    entrepreneurial enterprise, support
        of, xvi–xvii, 126–128, 130–131,
        135, 140, 141, 145–146
    federal government projects, broad
        ramifications of, 11, 12
    "for you" policy agenda and, xii–xiv,
        xvii, 12–13, 15, 18–22

    home visitation programs and, 30
    Houlahan childcare case and, 20–22
    immigration policy and, 13–14
    infant care initiatives and, 28–31
    infrastructure projects and, xv, 76–78,
        81, 85–86, 89–90, 91
    maternity leave policy and, 20–22
    nonpartisan solutions and, 19–20, 22
    Operation Breakthrough and, 41–42
    opportunity-centered policy agenda
        and, 14–15
    Opportunity Democrats, bold ideas
        of, xii–xvii, 13–15
    paid family leave policy and, 31–33
    parenting education initiatives and,
        28–31
    Providence Talks model and, 35–36
    public-private partnerships, role of,
        12, 71–72, 83–91, 95–97
    skills gap, closing of, xv, 49, 50–54
    "Smart City" transportation
        challenge and, 11–12
    social contract portability and, 101,
        103, 106, 108–110, 113, 114–117
    solutions, diverse stakeholders in,
        12, 13
    sustainable agenda/narrative and,
        12–13, 15, 19
    teacher compensation/duties and,
        55–57
    technology investments and, 12
    women in the workforce, absence of,
        20–25, 39–41
    working-/middle-class issues,
        attention to, 17–20, 122–124
    "workplace ghosts" problem and,
        23–25

See also Childcare issues; Education reform; Entrepreneur Agenda; Entrepreneurial enterprise; "For you" policy agenda; Infrastructure projects; New Democratic agenda; Portable Social Contract framework; Rebound politics; Social contract portability

Opportunity Zones, 150

OregonSaves program, 120

Oufkir, Abdelwahab, 70, 71

Paid family leave policy, 31–33

Paid medical leave programs, 121–122

Parenting education initiatives, 28–31

Parents as Teachers program, 30

Partnership BC model, 97

Partnerships. *See* Public-private partnerships

Pathways through Technology Early College High School (P-TECH) program, 61–63, 64

Peace Corps service, 160

Pennsylvania Rapid Bridge Replacement Program, 90–91

Pew Research Center, 107

Policy stagnation, 2–3, 4

American systems, unresponsiveness of, 6

big government gospel and, 4, 5, 7, 10

bureaucratic bloat/bungling and, 5–6, 7

defensive campaigns/governance and, 7

government-only/ideology-driven solutions and, 6–7, 8

messaging failure and, 5

obsolete professions, new directions and, 5

Republican provocation, response to, 9

See also New Democratic agenda

Port of Baltimore project, 88–89

Portable Benefits for Independent Workers Pilot Program Act, 121

Portable Social Contract framework, 115–116

Black Car Fund/workers compensation and, 117

construction workers/performers, centralized union benefits and, 117

employers/employees, beneficial ecosystem for, 123

"for you" policy agenda and, 118–124

gig economy safety net programs and, 118–122, 123–124

Individual Security Accounts system and, 118–119, 120, 121

national-level comprehensive benefits system and, 119, 121, 122

new vision of portable benefits and, 116–117, 123–124

opportunity-centered policy agenda and, 119, 122–124

OregonSaves program case example, 120

paid medical leave programs and, 121–122

portable benefits, politics of, 122–124

portable benefits principle of, xvi, 119–120

portable/prorated/universal benefits system and, 118–122

prorated costs, principle of, 120–121

state/local reforms, laboratories of democracy and, 119, 122

twenty-first century realities and,
119–124
unions, role of, 117
universal benefits principle of,
121–122
See also Social contract portability
Private enterprise. See Public-private
partnerships
Providence Public School District case,
59
Providence Talks model, 35–36
Public-private partnerships, 12
barriers to, 89, 94–97
bid-and-build system and, 93–94
bonded out projects and, 94–95
bridge repair work and, 90–91
COVID-19 pandemic, recovery
from, xv
education reform and, 71–72
efficiencies/benefits of, 96–97
examples of, 87–89, 92
federal grants and, 95
government support of, 95, 96–97
infrastructure projects and, xv, 83–91,
92, 93
New Deal programs and, 93
opportunity-centered policy agenda
and, 89–90, 95–97
Partnership BC model and, 97
Pennsylvania Rapid Bridge
Replacement Program and,
90–91
political obstacles to, 95
Port of Baltimore project and, 88–89
private sector partners, regulation
of, 89, 91
public cost in, 89, 95–96
public/private entities, combined
strengths of, 86–87, 89
social/economic justice goals and,
85–86

success, factors in, 88–89
taxpayers, protection of, 95–96
Public Works Administration (PWA), 93
Pursuit nonprofit organization, 69–71

"Race to the Top" initiative, 11
Racism, 14, 18
Raimondo, Gina, 59
Ranken Technical College case, 63–64
Read, Tobias, 120
Reagan, Ronald W., 7, 14
Rebound politics, 153
activism/grassroots interest,
awakening of, 163–164
at-risk voters, harnessing of, 158,
161–163
brand development tools/
organizations and, 161–162
bread-and-butter concerns,
addressing of, 157, 160
candidate development, bottom-up
experience and, 162, 163
Democratic electorate, segments of,
159
Democratic ideology, wide appeal of,
156, 159, 161–163, 164
Democratic messaging, positive
direction of, 156, 159, 160, 161,
163–164
Democratic-Republican differences,
highlighting of, 158, 161
entitlements, reconfiguration of, 161
far-left ideological political rhetoric
and, 155, 159
"for you" winning strategy and,
160–163
grassroots organizing and, 162–163,
164
Hidden Tribes project findings and,
159

kitchen-table issues, importance of,
157, 160
mutual support, network
development and, 162–163
national service, call to, 160–161, 163
opportunity-centered policy agenda
and, 155, 158, 161–163
partisan divide, bridging of, 155, 156,
158–159, 161–163
policy platform, expanded appeal of,
158, 162–163
pragmatic political approach and,
154, 155
reactive stance, move beyond, 155,
156, 160, 163–164
Republican/conservative ideology,
power of, 155–156, 161
Republican conservatives,
disenchantment with, 154, 155,
158
resource distribution, strategic
approach to, 162
service-oriented candidates and, 155
social issues, top-billing for, 157
Spanberger, Abigail, case example of,
153–155
state races, renewed interest/
investment in, 155, 162
swing voters, interest of, 155, 156,
158–159, 162–163
Trump-free political rhetoric and,
155–156
twenty-first century challenges,
sustainable solutions to, 164
2018 election and, 3, 76, 102, 156
2020 election strategy and, 159,
161–163
voter turnout, vital importance of,
158, 162
winning strategies and, 157–164

See also "For you" policy agenda; New
Democratic agenda; Opportunity
Agenda
Reinhardt, Emily, 150–151
Republican agenda, 1
childcare support, dismissal of,
40–41, 43–44
Democratic policy stagnation and,
2–3, 4, 9
growing government, opposition
to, 4
immigration policy and, 154
infrastructure, lack of interest in, 76
Opportunity Democrats, bold ideas
of, 13–15
opposition to, 2
paid family leave, opposition to, 31
provocation goal and, 9
Republican implosion, 2018 election
and, 3, 154
Social Security benefits, paring down
of, 109
tax cut legislation and, 77
women in the workforce, opposition
to, 25
See also Democratic renaissance;
Trump, Donald J.; 2016 election;
2018 midterm election; 2020
election
Retirement provisions, 106–110
Roosevelt, Franklin D., 93, 109
Ross, Shelton, 135–136
Rouhanifard, Paymon, 57–58
Run for Something, 163
Rural Business Development Grants,
149
Rural Microentrepreneur Assistance
Program, 149

Sailer, Sister Berta, 41
SAS software, 72
Save the Children, 29
Schmidt, Eugene, 67
Small Business Administration (SBA),
    132, 146–150
Small Business Committee, 138
Small Business Development Centers,
    148
Smart City Media, 84
"Smart City" transportation challenge,
    11–12
Social contract portability, 99
    American economic foundation,
        shift in, xvi, 103–106
    current work benefits/expectations
        and, 103–106
    defined-benefit vs. defined-
        contribution accounts and, 108,
        121
    employer-supported retirement
        benefits and, 108
    First Ascent Design case example,
        110–113
    General Motors workforce,
        approaches to, 99–100
    gig economy, move toward, 100–103
    gig freedoms, price of, 101–102,
        104, 105
    Great Recession, impact of, 100–101
    health care coverage portability and,
        115
    independent contracting, move
        toward, 101–102
    job lock paralysis, benefits
        maintenance and, 111–113
    labor insecurity and, 100–101, 104
    labor security and, 99–100, 103–104
    life expectancy, expansion of, 107
    Nissan factory case, 104–105

    opportunity-centered policy agenda
        and, 101, 103, 106, 108–110,
        113, 114–117, 122
    outsourcing practice and, 105
    portable benefits, new vision of, xvi,
        116–117
    retirement security, downturn in,
        106–110
    savings for retirement, inadequacy of,
        106, 107–108
    social contract, unraveling of,
        105–106, 109–110
    Social Security system, reshaping of,
        108–110
    temp agencies, outsourcing to, 105
    traditional full-time employment,
        benefits loss and, 105
    "Treaty of Detroit" case example and,
        114–115, 119, 122
    twentieth century workplace benefits,
        105, 113, 114–115, 119, 122
    twenty-first century economic
        flexibility and, 104–106
    twenty-first century workplace
        benefits and, 110–113
    unions, role of, 104–105, 114, 117
    well-being, erosion of, 104
    workplace benefits, loss of, 100–103,
        104, 105, 106, 108
    workplace benefits, portability of,
        103, 113, 114–117
    See also Opportunity Agenda;
        Portable Social Contract
        framework
Social justice issues, 7, 85–86, 136–137
Social media, 9, 159, 162, 164
Social Security system, 108–110
Spanberger, Abigail, 153–156
Sprint Wi-Fi network, 84

Stanford Center on Longevity, 106, 107
Suits, Nick, 62

TaskRabbit, 101, 115
Third Way think tank, 131, 133
Thorndike, Edward, 46
Time Warner service, 81–82, 84
"Treaty of Detroit," 114–115, 119, 122
Trump, Donald J., xii, 1, 2
    COVID-19 pandemic, leadership
        failures and, xii, xiii–xiv
    Democratic big government agenda
        and, 7
    immigration issue and, 13–14, 154
    infrastructure projects, opinion on,
        78–81
    negative reaction to, 1, 2, 3, 13, 15,
        156
    Opportunity Democrats, new
        generation of, 13, 14–15, 156
    racism/xenophobia and, 14, 78
    sexist rhetoric and, 78
    2016 election of, 2, 17, 44, 78–79
    2018 midterm election and, 3
    2020 election and, 13–15
    "We're losing" core message of,
        78–81
    See also 2020 election
2016 election
    Crawfordsville case and, 17
    Democratic governing philosophy,
        failure of, 2, 122–123, 125
    immigration issue and, 13–14
    income inequality issue and,
        125–126
    progressive agenda, defection from,
        122
    Trump's campaign rhetoric and,
        78–81, 161
    virtual tie in, 2

2018 midterm election
    Democratic resurgence and, 1–2, 3,
        76, 156
    Republican implosion and, 3, 154
2020 election
    anger, motivating factor of, 158
    Crawfordsville case and, 17
    Democratic governing philosophy
        and, 2–3, 159
    Trump's vulnerabilities, revelation
        of, 159
    See also New Democratic agenda;
        Opportunity Agenda; Rebound
        politics
Twitter, 157, 158, 162

Uber, 70, 101, 115, 116, 117, 120
US Department of Agriculture (USDA),
    149

Venture capitalists, 129–130, 134, 136,
    137
Veterans In Politics (VIP) program, 72
Village Capital, 136–137
Voters. See Electorate

Warner, Mark, 121
Weams, Bridgette, 64
"What Works Cities" initiative, 35
Whitmer, Gretchen, 76
Women, Infants, and Children (WIC)
    program, 23
Women's Business Centers, 148
Women's Empowerment Initiative, 32
Woodstock Institute, 140
Working-/middle-class issues
    American systems, unresponsiveness
        of, 6, 7

automation, jobs/benefits erosion
and, xvi
COVID-19 pandemic, economic
crisis and, xi–xiv, xvi–xvii
Crawfordsville case example and,
17–19
educational deficiencies and, 48–49
"for you" policy agenda and, 18–20
glass ceiling and, 24–25
Great Recession, impact of, 100–103
infrastructure improvement jobs and,
89–90
job lock paralysis and, 111–113
job opportunities, loss of, 79
modern benefits system,
development of, xvi
opportunity agenda and, xiv–xvii,
17–18
policy approaches and, 6–8, 9, 10–11
progressive Democratic agenda,
defection from, 122–123
purchasing power of wages and,
107–108
savings for retirement, inadequacy of,
106–108
skills gap and, 50–54
unemployment and, xvi
wage stagnation and, 107
women in the workforce and, 20–25,
39–41
workforce skill development
initiatives and, 5
"workplace ghosts" and, 23–25
See also Childcare issues; Economic
policy; Electorate; Entrepreneur
Agenda; Entrepreneurial
enterprise; "For you" policy
agenda; New Democratic agenda;
Opportunity Agenda; Portable
Social Contract framework;
Social contract portability

"Workplace ghosts," 23–25
Works Progress Administration (WPA),
93
World Bank, 51, 61

Xenophobia, 14

Young, Natalie, 133–135
Youth Service Corps, 161

Zivinsky, Andy, 135